«MORE THAN MEETS THE EYE»

The Foster Grant Story

"MORE THAN THE

Coronet Books

MEETS EYE»

THE FOSTER GRANT STORY

by
Glenn D. Kittler

"MORE THAN MEETS THE EYE": THE FOSTER GRANT STORY, *by Glenn D. Kittler*

First Printing: February, 1972

In Memorium

For many years, it was Joe Foster's dream that the history of Foster Grant would one day be written as a tribute to his father. Although there were one or two beginnings, the project never seemed to get very far. And then one day Sam Foster was gone.

The death of his father spurred Joe Foster into renewed efforts to publish the company's history; and it seemed fitting that the book be planned as an integral part of Foster Grant's fiftieth anniversary celebration in 1968–69.

Books seem to resist precise scheduling, however. The writing and editing processes somehow stretched out. Other, more urgent, matters kept arising. And then Joe Foster himself took ill.

It was hoped that this book would take final form in time for Joe Foster to see it. But it wasn't to be. He died in November, 1971, as this book was entering its final phase of production.

"More Than Meets The Eye" remains, as its subtitle suggests, "The Foster Grant Story," with emphasis on the good old days when Foster Grant was young and struggling. The book is, as Joe Foster wanted it to be, a tribute to Samuel Foster, Jr., who started it all in 1919.

Inevitably, the book is something more than that, something in addition to an affectionate glance over the corporate shoulder to the early days. It is, in the last analysis, a tribute to the second Foster of Foster Grant, who became captain of a small enterprise thirty years ago and steered it to bigness and national notice.

At an early stage of the writing of this book, someone suggested as a possible title—"The Son Also Rises." It was voted down, but it does seem remarkably apt.

Illustrations

1. SAMUEL FOSTER, JR., 1883–1966. Founder and First President, Foster Grant Co., Inc.
2. AN OLD TUNE: The former Richardson Piano Factory —now Foster Grant Co., Inc., in Leominster, as seen half a century ago.
3. KEY MACHINE: In 1930, Sam Foster brought over from Germany a new machine for injection molding of plastics. Foster Grant technicians made the machine commercially adaptable, permitting Foster Grant to become the first American company to adopt injection molding.

4. SHADES OF THE PAST: Remember these? Here's a collection of Foster Grant sunglasses, vintage 1940. Even then, Foster Grant was the world's largest sunglass manufacturer.

5. LET 'ER GO!: Joe Foster, sunglasses in hand, turns on production at Foster Grant's monostyrene plant in Baton Rouge, La. The year: 1954.

6. NUMBER ONE: The first of Foster Grant's own tank cars to arrive at Leominster from Baton Rouge, La. in the early 1950's.

7. GOVERNOR JOHN VOLPE of Massachusetts and screen star Carroll Baker joined Joe Foster at the 1966 dedication of The Samuel Foster Sunglass Plant in Leominster, the most modern production facility in the sunglass industry. Miss Baker was then starring in Foster Grant's "Sunglasses of the Stars" advertising campaign.

8. A TOAST: Joe Foster is toasted by Robert Siegfried, president of The Badger Company, Inc., during the 1969 groundbreaking ceremonies on the big new addition to the Foster Grant monostyrene production facility at Baton Rouge, La. Badger, one of the world's largest engineering and construction firms, built the plant addition.

9. BIG DAY: Joe Foster, joined by several Foster Grant directors and company officers, addresses a throng at the 1969 dedication of the Baton Rouge monostyrene plant.

10. VIVA RAQUEL!: The Raquel Welch advertisement for Foster Grant sunglasses, which appeared in *Life* Magazine, among other publications, was judged one of the best-read ads of 1968. And small wonder.

«MORE THAN MEETS THE EYE»

The Foster Grant Story

1

Irene Castle had her hair bobbed.

When this event occurred, it made headlines across the country, and it became the kickoff for the roaring Twenties. Some people thought it was charming. Some people thought it was daring. Some people thought it was shocking. To the people of Leominster, an industrial town in the heart of Massachusetts, it was downright catastrophic. The manufacture of combs and hair ornaments was the town's major industry, and Leominster was already known as America's Comb Capital. Now Irene Castle decided to cut her hair and Leominster was thrown into turmoil. Everybody knew that the women of the country would quickly follow the example of this beautiful celebrity who, with her husband Vernon, had become the leading exponent of ballroom dancing and the ultimate arbiter of how to dress while doing so. Overnight, half the comb factories in Leominster shut down. Thousands of people were suddenly out of work.

There was one man in Leominster who refused to let his life be ruined by the whimsical decision of this elegant hoofer. He was Samuel Foster, Jr. He was thirty-eight years old at the time. He was married, he had a teenage son, and every cent he owned was sunk into a new business he had recently started. He made combs and hair ornaments. As Leominster shook under the staggering blow struck by a delightful woman who was merely exercising her female prerogatives, Sam Foster calmly told his worried staff, "So all right. We'll make something else."

This calm, this ease for change, this refusal to be staggered by anyone or anything became the trademark of Samuel Foster, Jr. Starting out in a dingy shack jammed against a cliffside on Manning Avenue, Sam Foster began to build an empire at a time when other men were filing for bankruptcy. Today Sam Foster's name means more to more people than ever saw Irene Castle dance or even remember who she was. On that day in 1921 when Sam Foster decided to make something else, he took his first steps toward the creation of three major industries—sunglasses, injection molding, and plastics. By the time, in 1969, when Sam's little company was celebrating its Golden Anniversary, the tiny workshop on

Manning Avenue had developed into a huge complex of factories and processing plants across the country, and the staff of a dozen people had increased to twenty-two hundred. In 1921, Sam's firm—Foster Grant Co., Inc.—had a book value of about $20,000; in 1969, its value was over $35,000,000. And the end was not in sight.

In 1969, Sam's son Joseph, a youngster when Irene Castle had her hair bobbed, had become Chairman of the Board of the company whose products he once tried to sell door-to-door as a boy—an effort at which he had failed. But Joe Foster more than made up for this early misadventure. When he took over the management of the company from his father in 1942, Foster Grant was just reaching sales of $1 million a year. In the Golden Anniversary Year, the sales of Foster Grant products would surpass $70 million. The company which had started out as a small-town "family" operation had matured into a public corporation of significant leadership in its three fields of production. Its fifty years of steady growth were highlighted by repeated displays of originality, vision, and sound judgment in the areas of products, services, and marketing.

Yet, uniquely, the vast changes in the structure of Foster Grant in its fifty years nevertheless left the company's personality and character unchanged. Structurally, Foster Grant had changed from a jack-of-all-trades staff, to an impressive array of masters of their trades, some cultivated from the community, others attracted from around the world. Structurally, the company whose staff was once able to gather for lunch around a potbellied stove had developed into a company whose executives spent most of their time in the business capitals of the world in decisive consultation with the leaders of industry and science. And structurally, as a business entity, the Foster Grant of 1969 resembled the Foster Grant of 1919, even the Foster Grant of 1942, about as much as an Apollo spacecraft resembles a kite.

These changes came about as a result of ambitious teamwork and astute management. In the years immediately following World War II, Foster Grant had already become the world's largest manufacturer of sunglasses, the world's largest injection molder, and the world's largest user of polystyrene. Rather than content itself with further growth within these spheres, the company turned its attention as well to the challenging world of plastics production, first by making its own styrene polymer, then by making its own styrene monomer. This was a daring thing to do. The petrochemicals industry already had its giants, and they were not about to make room for a newcomer. The room was made, however, because of the approach the company took.

Foster Grant, as molders, first made itself its own best customer for plastics. Its fabricated articles had worldwide distribution and soon the world was seeing examples of new heights in quality for molded plastics. Then through a masterful combination of research and development, production and services, and sales and merchandising, Foster Grant became, by its Golden Anniversary Year, a giant among the giants.

The ambitious teamwork and astute management which brought this about have always been at the heart of the Foster Grant spirit. Internally, the company has remained a family operation. Over the years, it has been common for two,

4

even three, generations of the same family to be at work together in various departments of the company. Strangers have come from other places, met at Foster Grant, and married. At its Golden Anniversary, the company's Twenty-Five-Year Club had a hundred and fifty-seven members with a total service of over six thousand years. One member—Grace Goodale—had been the company's first employee, fifty years before. And a member of the Board of Directors had been Joe Foster's partner in their teenage effort to become door-to-door salesmen.

Something more than loyalty has been a part of this. There has been involvement. In the early days, Foster Grant people had a sense of belonging simply because their jobs made them so interdependent. Production was by hand, with several people working on each comb, each piece of costume jewelry, each decorative article, with each item becoming the product of a group effort. There had to be a certain individual pride involved. No man or woman would pass on a piece of work without the confidence of having contributed creatively to its quality. Out of this developed a sense of responsibility, each worker to his job, each worker to his fellow workers, all workers to the company, to Sam and Joe Foster, and Sam and Joe Foster, in return, to the workers. Later on, especially during the company's surge forward into petrochemicals, new types of men were needed, men with valuable experience in the field, and young men about to leave college and begin their careers in it. Meeting this need brought many new faces into the company, but with them came the same spirit. Suddenly expanded teamwork became the company's breath of survival in a fiercely competitive industry.

Foster Grant veterans who had brought the company to this point had priceless know-how to offer the recruits. And the recruits, many of them already with a special know-how of their own, guided the company to its present leadership in the industry.

In the course of this progress, an important "first" occurred. Foster Grant, widely acknowledged as the leading molder of plastic articles, took a step "backwards" in the manufacturing process by becoming producers of the basic materials. Not only was this a "first"—it was also an "only." No other company has been in a position to do the same. Since this development, other giants in petrochemicals have adopted a similar policy, but from the opposite direction—they have acquired subsidiaries to use their basic materials. Approaching the expansion the way Foster Grant did put the company in a decisively advantageous position. It was as though a tailor who had won fame for the quality of his suits had begun making his own cloth, and in order to sell his cloth to other tailors, he invited them into his shop so that they could learn for themselves how to make better suits. The Foster Grant facilities thus became a big laboratory for the molding industry. Sometimes other molders brought their dies into the Foster Grant plant to experiment with Foster Grant plastics on the company's machines. Sometimes Foster Grant experts went into another molder's plant and showed him how to get the best from Foster Grant plastics on his own equipment. Either way, there was a display here of the trust which the molding competitors had in the Foster Grant people. Ordinarily, a businessman does not reveal his manufacturing secrets or his production plans to the competition.

However, the other molders knew they could trust the Foster Grant people. This was—and still is—a rare occurrence in business. At Foster Grant, however, this kind of respect for the customer and this kind of customer trust in Foster Grant have been characteristic of the company since its first days.

* * * *

When Samuel Foster, Jr., first heard of Leominster, Massachusetts, he wasn't sure where it was. That was in 1907. Sam was living in Providence, Rhode Island, then; he was twenty-four years old; he was married; his son Joe was four years old. Sam was working for the George W. Dover Company, manufacturers of costume jewelry, and he was a foreman of one of the departments. It was at Dover's that Sam met Jennie Probis, whom he married.

Sam Foster went to work at Dover's without knowing a thing about jewelry making. But this was typical of him. All his life, he never hesitated to move into a new area just because he didn't know anything about it. He knew he could learn. He also knew that there were always men around who knew enough to get the thing started. Sam's special genius was to devise new ways to do the thing better, easier, and cheaper.

The Foster family were Jewish immigrants who arrived in the United States from Austria in 1897, when Sam was fourteen. A daughter—Augusta—was also born in Europe. The rest of the Foster children—sons Maurice and Harry and daughters Rose, Pauline, and Tillie—were born here. Like so many immigrant families that flocked to America at the turn of the century, the Fosters arrived with no money but with rich hopes. Sam Foster, Sr., was not a young man. Breaking old ties and old ways in the old country had been difficult for him. But he wanted his children to have a future, and he knew there would be no real future for them in Europe. The age-old tradition of remaining at the social and economic level at which you were born, no matter what talents you had, shut all doors to a real future, especially for the poor. Sam, Sr., had spent all of his adult life saving for the fare to America.

The Fosters stayed in New York City a short while and then went north to Providence, where Sam, Sr., had a cousin, with whom they stayed briefly. Then came the task of finding jobs. Because the family had nothing, it became necessary for both parents and their son to go to work. They took what jobs they could get. Because they could scarcely speak English, they found themselves in the most menial positions in factories or shops. For Sam, Jr., a formal education was over, except for the study of English. Throughout his life, Sam Foster never lost the pleasant Austrian accent of his English. Sam was small as a boy, and serious. Even in manhood, he did not grow beyond five feet five, but as he matured he acquired a firm, stocky body that seemed to give him more height than he had. Sam matured into a gentle man, pleasant, soft-spoken, easy-going, kind and considerate and generous, and he never visibly lost his temper. Years later, Billy Moran, one of Sam's first employees, said of him, "If you ever heard Sam say as much as 'For heaven's sake!' you knew he was mad."

8

The Fosters had been in Providence about two years when they got the opportunity to operate a grocery store on a rental basis, with an option to buy. For two years, they put in fourteen-hour days behind the counters, except on the Sabbath, which they observed by closing the store even though it was the busiest shopping day in the neighborhood. The work was hard; the days seemed endless. Even after closing, there were two or three more hours of work to do—cleaning the place, re-stocking the shelves, planning orders for salesmen who would arrive early in the morning. When the day came to decide about the option, they decided against it. The grinding toil had taken its toll on the health of Sam, Sr., and clearly he could not take much more of it. In fact, he was never again able to do anything but the lightest work.

It was about this time that Sam, Jr., began to show his mettle. As a new American, Sam grasped the historical significance of the Fourth of July, but, as a boy, the best part of the holiday for him was the fireworks, with the city exploding around him. By the time he was approaching seventeen, however, he no longer considered himself a boy. After all, his mother and he were now the principal breadwinners of the family, and he knew that her working days were numbered. Thus he was always alert for some new way to earn a little more money. An aspect of Independence Day that had impressed him was the obvious fortune that people threw away just for the fun of making a lot of noise. As another Fourth neared, Sam began giving this aspect increasing thought.

Through inquiries, he learned that most of the fireworks

in Providence were manufactured in Boston and distributed locally through wholesalers. He also learned that there were many towns in New England that had to obtain their supplies by mail order because they were too remote or too small for wholesalers to service. This stirred Sam's gift for business. He found out that the wholesalers' mark-up was too small for him to buy from them and then compete against them with the retailers in those towns. Inventive by nature, he decided to start from scratch and make his own fireworks and then do his own selling direct to the retailers. He specialized in torpedoes. These were one-inch paper tubes, about the girth of a nickel; they contained an explosive and had a cap at each end. When thrown forcefully against a hard surface, they resounded sharply. They were very popular. Sam obtained a few torpedoes and took them apart carefully to see how they were made. Then he bought supplies and began making his own. His product was first-rate. Early in June, he headed for New England. He did very well. The next year, he did even better. But the next year, he ran into some tough luck. Sam worked in a shed behind his house, and one night a spark accidentally fell upon a batch of the explosive. Sam got outside just in time to turn around and watch the roof of the shed go soaring into the air in splinters. During the fire that broke out, the finished torpedoes started popping off like machine-gun fire, sending the whole neighborhood on the run for a premature Fourth of July celebration. After the excitement died down, Sam realized that his loss was too great for a fresh start, and that was the end of that.

It was during this period that Sam got a job as a waiter in a Providence restaurant. Because he was quick, quiet, amiable, and efficient, the customers liked him, and people began asking for one of his tables when they came in. The owner, impressed by this, decided that Sam could be even more effective as the headwaiter. Thus Sam Foster became a maître d' while still a teenager. Even at that age, Sam deplored waste of any kind, including the waste of space. One evening as he was surveying the crowded room, he found himself thinking that a lot of money-earning space was being wasted because the tables were badly arranged. Next evening, he arrived at work early, and when the owner came in, he saw Sam just finishing the job of rearranging the room. Sam said, "See? Now you've got space for six or seven more tables." This time, Sam's initiative did not impress the owner, probably because he hadn't thought of the idea himself. Sam just had time to put the tables back where they were before customers started to arrive. Perhaps it was Sam's lingering impatience with waste that led him to decide to bring an end to this venture of his life. And this led him to Dover's.

Sam's youngest brother, Harry, also went to work at Dover's. As close as all the Foster children were, Sam and Harry were particularly close and remained so for life. The Dover company was doing well and, after a couple of years, moved to larger quarters. Sam made the move, but Harry did not. Harry enjoyed designing jewelry more than just piecing it together, and so he went with another company where he felt he would have a better opportunity to pursue his own interests. He was there when, in 1907, Sam told him about a job offer in Leominster.

Harry said, "Combs, Sam? You don't know anything about combs."

Sam shrugged. "I didn't know anything about jewelry when I went to work at Dover's. I can learn. Harry, I want you to come along. I want you to work with me."

"In combs, Sam? I'm a jewelry designer."

"I know," said Sam, "but it won't do you any harm to learn something new. Besides, I'm not asking you to make a career out of combs. I just thought it would be enjoyable to have you around for a while, at least until Jennie and I get settled."

Harry understood. "All right, Sam." The day would come when Harry Foster would cross the continent to be with Sam just because Sam said he had something he wanted to talk to him about.

*　*　*　*

Comb-making as a business began in America around 1760 in the town of West Newbury, Massachusetts, in the northeast corner of the colony. Local farmers usually turned to some craft to earn money in winter, and a number of them made combs. Enoch Noyes was reportedly the first of them to do well enough at it to progress to comb-making on a year-round basis, which he did for twenty years. Combs were made from buffalo horn and tortoise shell, both abundantly available, but the workmanship was crude because of the lack of skill and proper tools. Quality combs continued to come from England for another hundred years.

Comb-making was started at Leominster in 1775 by Obediah Hills, whose family had moved there the year before from West Newbury. Presumably, Obediah and his brother Silas had learned how to make combs in the shop of Enoch Noyes. Leominster, incorporated in 1740, had a population of less than a hundred when the Hills arrived, and the area was given mostly to farming and cattle breeding. By then, comb-makers had learned that cattle horn was a better substance for combs than buffalo horn, cheaper and more manageable. At Worcester, just twenty miles to the south, there was already a sizable abattoir, providing a good source of supply. Within a year after the Hill brothers began their work at Leominster, six or seven other comb-makers moved there from West Newbury, and Leominster was on its way.

By 1850, Leominster was turning out two-thirds of the combs then being manufactured in the country every year. The town had twenty-eight comb companies, employing four hundred people, and doing an aggregate business of $275,-000 a year.

Two developments in the years following the Civil War gave the comb industry great impetus. One was a new technique for using rubber for combs, greatly cutting down the cost. The other was the development of Celluloid, the world's first plastic. Celluloid was invented by John W. Hyatt, a pressman living in Albany, New York, in 1868. A billiard buff, Hyatt learned that billiard balls were becoming increasingly expensive and rare because of a shortage of ivory. In fact, the shortage was so serious that Phelan and Collander, manufacturers of billiard balls, had offered $10,000 to anybody who could produce a substitute for natural ivory. Whether Hyatt ever collected this money is not known, but soon after he put Celluloid on the market, he didn't need the award.

The man knew his chemistry. And he had done his homework. He knew that a number of European scientists were trying to produce new substances from cellulose, the main ingredient of cell walls in plants, especially cotton and wood, but they weren't having much luck. Using cellulose nitrate, camphor, and alcohol under heat and pressure, Hyatt had a great deal of luck. Not only was Celluloid an excellent ivorylike coating for billiard balls, but Hyatt promptly started a dental company and used his invention for the manufacture of false teeth.

In Leominster, meanwhile, comb manufacturers were facing a shortage of their own: a shortage of cattle horns. The industry had continued to grow. Leominster had to be the obvious headquarters for anybody wanting to make combs because of the town's pool of skilled labor. Thus new companies were always being formed, with older companies merging or selling out at good profits. Each manufacturer did his own shopping for horn, and as the industry steadily grew, the time came when New England abattoirs could not meet the great demand. Only a few of the companies were big enough to send buyers to the slaughterhouses in other parts of the country. Others simply had to compete on the available market, and it was not uncommon for these companies to be weeks, even months, behind on their orders because of the shortages.

To overcome the problem, the owners of several of these companies joined together to form The Horn and Supply Company, a move which enabled them to send buyers across the country to purchase horns in quantity. Besides selling to member-manufacturers, the company sold to anybody else in town who needed horn. With time, the horn shortage became a national problem, so the company sent its buyers to Europe. As it turned out, the European horn was not of good quality, so the company sent its buyers to South America. One of the buyers for The Horn and Supply Company was Bernard W. Doyle, a native of Leominster, a graduate of the Leominster High School in 1891 and of the Eastman Commercial College at Poughkeepsie, New York, two years later. His first job after college was with Horn and Supply, and he was soon sent on the road, here and abroad, as a buyer. In 1897, he became secretary and manager of the company. An expert on horn, he knew that the day was not far off when the scarcity of horn would cause a serious economic crisis in his home town, and so he began to look around for something else.

By then, two or three Leominster comb manufacturers were experimenting with Celluloid, and they liked it. The trouble was that they couldn't get much of it. In just a few years, so many different uses had been found for Celluloid that production was far behind the demand. It was far less expensive and much more workable than horn, shell, ivory, amber, mother of pearl, rubber. Easily softened in hot water, it could be stretched into any form or shape, and it hardened quickly. If you made a mistake, you just softened it again and started over. It could be sawed, drilled, turned, planed, buffed, and polished. It would take colors. It came in sheets, rods, and tubes.

Bernard Doyle was impressed. Besides being associated with The Horn and Supply Company, Doyle was also treasurer of the Paton Manufacturing Company. Alexander Paton, a Scotsman, arrived in Leominster in 1871, at the age of seventeen, and went to work in the comb industry. At twenty-five, he started his own company. In 1897, Paton was elected president of the Horn and Supply cooperative, which brought him into close contact with Doyle. That same year, Paton incorporated his own firm, and he invited Doyle to join his staff. It was around 1900 that Doyle went to Paton with an idea. Following their discussion, Doyle also presented the idea to Ludwig Stross, an officer of Albert Ochse and Company, the largest horn dealers in the world. Next, Doyle talked to Paul Rie, of Paris, France, the leading French importer of South American horn and owner of a Paris comb company.

It was obvious to Bernard Doyle that Celluloid was going to become a major material in the comb and hair ornaments industries, so he proposed to his three friends that they should all join to establish a new company which would produce its own celluloid-like substances for its own use and for sale to the industry at large. The three men agreed. The plastic they were making within a year was given the trade name of Viscoloid. Their company: The Viscoloid Company, with Bernard Doyle as president and treasurer. The Viscoloid Company promptly became a giant in the industry, eventually occupying sixty-two buildings on forty acres of land in Leominster. From its own plastic, the company made dressing combs, hairpins, hair ornaments, toys, brushes, mirrors, cutlery, toilet articles—the list was endless.

In 1907, The Viscoloid Company found itself in need of a new supervisor for the department of its comb division in which decorations of various kinds were affixed to the combs, and so the company placed an ad in a number of New England newspapers. Among those who saw the ad was Samuel Foster, Jr., of Providence.

You say *LEMmunster*. One day, a Foster Grant executive, in California on business, was putting through a call to the home office. In the past, he'd had some difficulty with long-distance operators who couldn't find LEMmunster in their directories, so this time he said: "I want to call Lee-oh-minster, Massachusetts." The operator said: "You mean LEMmunster." Pleased but taken aback, he said: "Right, but how did you know that?" She said: "That's my home town." He said: "It's mine, too, now." One way or another, this sort of exchange takes place practically every day somewhere in the country.

It is surprising, really—and yet not surprising at all—that a New England industrial community of just thirty thousand population should achieve such unique renown. Certainly, Leominster industry has been primarily responsible for this. In the Foster Grant Golden Anniversary Year, there *were* about one hundred thirty-five manufacturing firms in Leominster, employing some seven thousand people on an annual payroll of over thirty-five million dollars. This *was* tremendous economic health for a town this size, *or even for a* town twice the size. In terms of employees, payroll and business-volume, Foster Grant was far and away the leader in Leominster, its products the best known across the country. But there *were* other famous name-products in town. Arrow shirts. DuPont toothbrushes Standard Tool molds, Borden chemicals, and Selig furniture.

Like Foster Grant, some of these companies have production centers elsewhere, resulting in two-way traffic that helps to spread the name of Leominster. Again, like Foster Grant, some of these companies operate on an international basis, so Leominster is as well known to industry in Melbourne or Johannesburg or London or Tokyo as it is in Boston. It is, for example, a daily occurrence to hear three or four foreign languages being spoken in the Foster Grant reception rooms as customers, engineers, and salesmen from around the world gather for appointments with Foster Grant executives.

Another factor in Leominster's fame has been nearby Fort Devens. During World War II, servicemen from all over the country arrived here for their basic training, for maneuvers, for shipment overseas, returning here for their discharge from the military. During the war, Leominster experienced a severe labor shortage, and hundreds of servicemen received permission to work part-time in factories, many of them at Foster Grant, to help meet the pressing demands of wartime production. In this way they came to know Leominster families; in this way they came to know the Leominster girls they married, sometimes settling here, sometimes taking their wives back home, which was probably the case with the California long-distance operator.

Such circumstances place Leominster in a unique position. The city's young people know they can earn a good living in their home town and thus there is little of the exodus which has drained so many smaller cities and towns of their young and of their future. For Leominster, this means the retention of youngsters for whom a genius at machinery seems to be second nature. Also, the town's college graduates know they will be snapped up by local industry and be destined for important roles in management. As new techniques in industry and new discoveries in science created the need for people of special skills, Leominster leaders sought them out on campuses and in other industrial capitals. The blend of this new elite and the industrious townspeople has resulted in a cosmopolitan atmosphere that is unusual for a community this size. It is an atmosphere that keeps the city bustling with new ideas, new products, new horizons. In important ways, Foster Grant has spearheaded this creative drive ever since Sam Foster first came here over sixty years ago.

2

Sam Foster made his first trip to Leominster alone, for his interview at Viscoloid, and he was hired. His salary: twenty-five dollars a week, which was rather good in those days. Then he looked around for a place to live, and he had his troubles. The Leominster population was then around eight thousand, an increase of some thirty percent since the founding of The Viscoloid Company, and people were still moving into town faster than housing could be built for them. It was not uncommon for the breadwinner of a family to be living in a Leominster rooming house, with the rest of his family in another town, sometimes miles away, sweating out the Leominster housing crises.

Sam Foster was able to find two adjoining rooms in a private home, one furnished as a bedroom, the other as a living room, with communal kitchen and bath facilities down the hall. Next time Sam traveled to Leominster, his wife and son and brother were with him. Harry Foster was awarded the bedroom for himself; Sam, Jenny, and Joe slept in the living room. Harry Foster also went to work at Viscoloid, but he remained at Leominster just a year. Eager to get on with his own career as a designer of jewelry, he went back to Providence.

By 1910, Sam Foster had found a better home for his family, in the first-floor apartment of a two-flat building, and Sam was in the process of buying the building. This was in keeping with the aspiration that was so prevalent among immigrants flocking to America in those days. In Europe, it had been next to impossible for the average man to become a property-owner. Most private land had been held by the same rich families for generations, and often a tenant's occupancy of a house or a farm depended solely on the whims of the landlord. For these poor people, an important feature of life in America was the right to work hard and save money and one day own their own homes. Always they advised friends and relatives who followed them over from Europe, "Get to own your own home as soon as possible and you'll always have a place to live." Many of these families made great sacrifices during their first few years in the country in order to make this dream come true.

Property-ownership had another value for Sam Foster. He enjoyed real estate deals. After paying off his own home, Sam bought adjoining lots and put up three more two-flats. In the years ahead, Sam was to engage in real estate deals involving millions of dollars. He was to admit, one day, that he felt like kicking himself for not buying the Ambassador Hotel in Los Angeles, when it was available to him for $1.7 million—three years later, it sold to a hotel chain for close to $4 million. Still standing in Leominster is evidence of Sam's earlier efforts: Foster Court, a quadrangle of two-story apartments. Sam didn't claim to have any special knowledge of architecture, but he could never resist sidling up to an architect bent over blueprints and mildly suggesting, "That's very nice, but what do you think of moving the bathroom in this apartment over here? That way, it would back against the kitchen in the next apartment, and then it would be easier to put in the plumbing for both apartments, wouldn't it?"

Everybody liked Sam Foster. He met strangers easily. He was the sort of man toward whom other men could comfortably feel love and openly admit to it. People were always confiding in Sam, telling him their troubles; but if he ever had any troubles of his own, he kept them to himself. He was a private man. He listened well, usually not saying much, and often his attention seemed to have a soothing nature that made people feel better for having spoken to him.

His work was his life. Viscoloid, like most Leominster plants, usually operated from eight to five, with a half-day on Saturdays, but in the autumn rush to fill Christmas orders there were night shifts and full Saturdays, sometimes full Sundays. Sam was always in his workshop an hour ahead of everybody else, still there an hour and more after the others had left, and during the rush season he was there as long as a man or woman remained at a workbench. Sam was not a desk man; he had no mind for paperwork; he had too much energy to sit still for long. About fifty people worked for him at Viscoloid, and he preferred to be among them, moving from person to person, observing, suggesting, complimenting. Sam Foster was an idea man, and no matter how smoothly production might be going, he could always think of some way to make it go better. Often he would start a day with: "I was thinking last night, and I was wondering. . . ." And people would sit back and listen, knowing that once again Sam had come up with something new. Always it was something better.

* * * *

The thriving Viscoloid Company brought prosperity to Leominster, not only through its own production but also through the work it provided other companies in town by jobbing out part of its production. Perhaps this was what encouraged Sam Foster to go into business for himself. Actually, Sam Foster was by nature the sort of man who could only be content in a business of his own. He needed full responsibility for a job to be able to derive the fullest satisfaction from it. His job at Viscoloid covered just one part of comb-making, which for Sam was like sitting down to just part of a meal. He needed more than that. In May, 1919, he went after it.

Sam's first employee was Grace Goodale and, despite

the warnings of her friends, she was glad to take the risk. Miss Goodale had worked at Viscoloid part-time while she was in high school and then, upon her graduation in 1910, went full-time. She had already worked for Sam for nine years. Any fears she might have had that the job might be short-lived did not materialize: Grace Goodale worked for Sam—and then for Joe Foster—for a total of forty-nine years.

The Foster Manufacturing Company began its life in a small building on Manning Avenue that had formerly been a laundry. Adjacent was a small house which Sam used as an office and for inventory. An embankment rose sharply behind the property, making the workshop all the darker. Occasionally rats came in from the nearby fields, bringing squeals from Grace Goodale and the nine other young women Sam had hired, and also bringing Sam on the run with a broom. The shop was an oven in summer and an icebox in winter and a sieve in a rainstorm at any time of the year. The equipment was primitive and the workmanship not much better. Because Viscoloid, like all the pyroxylins, was highly inflammable, the girls worked with a bucket of water at their side. The advent of Sam Foster's career as a man in business for himself was hardly glamorous and not very optimistic.

Sam soon found out that the work he expected to have jobbed to him by Viscoloid and other manufacturers in town was not always enough to enable him to meet his payroll, so he decided to bring out a few items of his own. He began with costume jewelry—flowers to be worn as pins or boutonnieres. First, the tiny "petals" had to be hand-sawed from the sheets of plastic. Then each flat petal had to be warmed enough for a worker to bend the softened substance to shape.

24

Then the petals had to be affixed to a base, either with glue or a thin wire, to form a flower. The next task was to sell the thing. Sometimes Sam went to stores in Boston or Providence or New York to make his own pitch. Sometimes buyers strolled the back streets of Leominster, looking for bargains from the smaller companies.

Sam knew he needed an experienced salesman. Handling sales himself took him out of the shop too much. Not only did Sam prefer working in the shop, but it was while he was in the shop that he was able to guard the quality of workmanship so that his products were saleable. On a visit to Providence, Sam talked about his need to Harry. By then, Harry had started his own jewelry manufacturing company, making mostly solid gold items, and he was selling to the better jewelry shops and department stores. And Harry said, "Well, Sam, I do know a good salesman who is shopping around. But I don't think he is looking for just another job. Last time I saw him, he said he might be interested in buying into a small company and taking over its sales department. Would you consider a partner, Sam?"

Sam would. And so it was in this way that Sam Foster met William Grant and that the Foster Manufacturing Company became the Foster Grant Company, Inc. But the partnership was short-lived. Looking back, Joseph Foster has said, "I don't know whether Bill Grant couldn't sell my father's line or whether Dad didn't turn out anything Bill Grant could sell. In either case, the partnership only lasted three or four months." The parting was amicable. When Grant withdrew from the company, Sam returned his investment, and this left Sam too financially strapped to pay for the legal process of having the corporate name changed, so he left the name of his company as it was. Thus Grant remained part of Foster Grant, a household name in 1969, even though Bill Grant had been active in the company for just a few months during a bleak period in 1920.

Unknown to Sam Foster, the sun was about to start shining for him. Responsible for this were Abraham and Jacob Goodman. In 1907, their father, Henry, had organized H. Goodman and Sons, merchandisers of combs and hair ornaments under the brand name of Goody. The Goodmans manufactured part of their line and purchased sub-assemblies from other producers. These parts were assembled and decorated at the Goodmans' shop (then at 648 Broadway, in New York), then marketed. Their biggest item was a three-piece set—a comb, a hairbrush, and a mirror, all decorated with rhinestones. As the two brothers gradually took over management of the company, Abe became the inside man, running the New York operation, and Jack was on the road selling. Sales were mostly to small jewelry stores, women's shops, and a few department stores.

The post-war years after World War I brought a business boom to the country. The Goodmans, already a going concern, were doing very well. On the road, Jack Goodman had finally succeeded in selling a couple of the Goody items to a syndicated chain, the S. S. Kresge Company at its Detroit headquarters, thus opening all the Kresge regional offices for the Goodmans. One day a Kresge buyer told Jack he was having trouble getting a certain item he felt would sell well: dice with rhinestones as markings instead of the usual darkened spots. Since the Goodmans worked with rhinestones, could they make the dice? Even without being sure, Jack said yes, and he rushed back to New York to present the job to Abe.

At the time, there were four companies in the East that made dice, usually out of bone or, when it was available, ivory. The Goodmans canvassed them all, and there was a problem. The Kresge people wanted dice of a small size, and boring holes in bone and ivory deep enough to imbed rhinestones caused these substances to chip and crack. Then somebody suggested the Viscoloid plastic, and it worked. The Kresge buyer was delighted with the finished item and ordered great quantities. And the transaction opened the Kresge door to the rest of the Goody line. The Goodmans were already successful. Now they moved into the big time and, they soon learned, their present suppliers of parts could not meet the new production demands.

The use of the Viscoloid plastic for the dice had brought The Viscoloid Company into the Goodman horizon. Late in 1920, Jack Goodman made his first trip to Leominster, intending to turn his company's business over to this industrial giant. Jack went by train from New York to Worcester, then covered the remaining twenty miles to Leominster by trolley car, which turned out to be a trip for daredevils only. As the car raced across the open fields, it swayed furiously on its tracks, like some monster struggling to escape from its leash. Then the car screeched to a halt in one small town after another and at crossings, sending people and packages skittering forward. The car was cold; its lights were temperamental; its frame rattled and wheezed threateningly. When Jack Goodman finally stepped down from the car, in Monument

Square, Leominster, a prayer on his lips, relief in his heart, he was quite sure he had reached the edge of the earth. A look around confirmed this. A week-old snow had been turned black by the town's many chimneys. It was twilight, making the square gloomier, and whatever constituted a rush hour in 1920 downtown Leominster was over, leaving a pall upon the place. Other passengers from the trolley disappeared into the darkness as though by black magic. Jack saw a boy across the street and went to him and asked, "Where is the best hotel in town?"

The boy jerked a thumb over his shoulder. "Right here."

Jack glanced at the decrepit building. He asked, "What makes you think so?"

The boy said, "My father runs it."

Jack felt he had no choice. The rest of Leominster seemed to have left town. He went in, signed the register, and carried his own luggage up to his room. Looking around, he would have believed anyone who told him that Christopher Columbus had slept here. He spent a sorry night.

Early the next morning, Jack Goodman headed for The Viscoloid Company, and bad news awaited him. Despite the company's size, its facilities were already overtaxed and they could take no more work. Rather than write the trip off as a total loss, Goodman called on other companies of the same size, and he was told the same thing. A couple of companies were willing to take the order, but they admitted they would probably job most of it out to small manufacturers in town. Because of the importance of the Kresge account, Jack did not want to take any chances on the smaller companies without first examining them. Equipped with a list, he began a tour of the town's back streets. Some of the companies were rejected by him because of their equipment, some because of the quality of the work they showed him; one or two he checked off as possibles.

It was mid-afternoon when Jack Goodman found himself turning into muddy Manning Avenue. Just ahead was a small, dark, dank building that looked as though it was debating whether to collapse. Across the face of it was a sign: FOSTER GRANT CO., INC. On an adjacent smaller building was another sign: OFFICE. Jack Goodman debated whether to bother, and then he went in. A young woman glanced up pleasantly and inquiringly from her typewriter. Jack Goodman said, "I'd like to see Mr. Grant, please."

She said, "Mr. Grant is no longer with us."

Jack asked, "Then who's running the place?"

"Mr. Foster."

"Oh." Thus Jack Goodman learned that Foster and Grant were two people. "Is Mr. Foster around, then?"

That moment, Sam came in from the plant, heard the question, and said, "I'm Sam Foster. What can I do for you?"

They talked into the twilight hours, appraising each other. Jack Goodman could tell that Sam Foster was a man who knew what he was talking about. After examining the Goody items, Sam said yes, he could make them, and Jack Goodman believed him. What Goodman had difficulty believing was that Sam's equipment was as good as the man himself. They had walked through the shop twice. In Jack's opinion, the place was a medieval dungeon. And yet the workmanship was good, some of it very good, and Jack Goodman concluded that such work could come out of such equipment only because of Sam Foster's demand for quality and his know-how for achieving it. At the same time, Sam Foster could tell that Jack Goodman was a man who knew what he was talking about. Goodman was direct and specific, and his comments about his own line, as well as Sam's production, clearly indicated that he would not settle for anything but the best. Sam felt it would be a pleasure to do business with a man like that.

Jack Goodman decided to take the risk. They discussed price and, Goodman knew, Sam's prices were fair. Jack gave Sam a test order. Then Goodman did some mental arithmetic regarding a deposit, and he asked, "How much do you want on deposit, Mr. Foster?"

Sam said, "Deposit? What deposit? You have given me an order. I'll make the merchandise. I'll ship it to you. I'll mail you a bill. You'll pay it."

Goodman said, "You are a very trusting man, Mr. Foster." There was a hint of reprimand in his voice.

Sam shrugged. "Mr. Goodman, you know better than I do if I can trust you. Can't I?"

Jack laughed. "Yes, Sam, you can trust me." And they shook hands on it. Jack glanced at his watch. "What time is the next trolley to Worcester, Sam? I'd like to head back to New York tonight."

"At six in the morning," Sam said.

Jack winced. "That means another night at the miserable hotel."

"Is it that bad?"

Jack said: "I've traveled all over the country, Sam, and this hotel takes the prize for misery."

"All right, then," Sam said. "You'll stay at my house to-night." And he waved away Jack's mild resistance.

During the year that followed, Foster Grant manufactured one third of the production the Goodman brothers ordered out of Leominster. The next year, Foster Grant did two thirds of the production. And by the third year, Foster Grant had it all. Moreover, news of the Foster Grant quality spread quickly in New York, and other customers began to appear.

Early in this turn of events, Sam Foster realized he needed an experienced and responsible man to work closely with him. Not all the new customers were as dauntless as Jack Goodman, who made regular trips on the trolley car and then to Sam's house, and so it became increasingly necessary for Sam to meet company representatives at places more convenient for them—Boston, Providence, Worcester, New York. Because these meetings usually involved negotiations, Sam felt his own presence was necessary, and thus he needed someone who could run the shop while he was away.

Looking around town, Sam chose a man named Fred England. England, an older man, had considerable supervisory experience with other companies in Leominster, and he could just about name his price anywhere in town. England's wife was a school teacher in Leominster, was also getting on in years, and the two of them were thinking of retiring. It was because of these circumstances that Fred England reacted favorably to a suggestion which Sam Foster made to him late in 1921. The offer: a good salary, a percentage of the profits, and the right to buy a full partnership in the company at any time. England accepted, but he did not enter the partnership for over two years because of his indecision about actually retiring. The partnership lasted for approximately two more years, when the prospect of retirement brought about its dissolution, but England stayed with Foster Grant for another year. The two men complemented each other well. Their contemporaries who were still with Foster Grant in its Golden Anniversary Year remembered England as a first-rate plant manager who was as insistent as Sam Foster on quality production. They remembered England, too, as a "typical Yankee," a bit withdrawn, laconic, but always amiable. During the partnership, Sam was willing to change the name of the company to Foster England, but it was Fred England who pointed out that the name of Foster Grant was becoming well known in the industry, and he was satisfied to let the name remain Foster Grant.

Even with Fred England on the job, Sam continued to spend most of his time at the plant in the workshop, never losing his intense interest in production. Though production was dedicated mostly to making parts for other companies, Sam continued to develop new products and thus kept adding to his own line. One of Sam's successful ideas was a plastic canary on a swinging perch in a plastic cage, four inches by six. The item was so successful from the start that Sam had to obtain another building, on Spruce Street, where eight men assembled the cages from parts made on Manning Avenue, and production averaged fifteen gross a day for almost five years.

Sam had another clever idea which, due to a certain fact of life, unfortunately never took off. It was a plastic handle for a woman's umbrella. About seven inches long, it was made from plastic strips, a half-inch wide, which, softened, were intertwined and looked like lattice work. It was very attractive and undoubtedly would have sold well as it was, but it was not good enough in a utilitarian sense for Sam Foster. So he asked himself: Besides trying to keep dry in the rain, what is next important to a woman? Her appearance. So Sam had the base of the handle put on a hinge, turning it into a cap, and in the base of this cap he placed a mirror slightly larger than a quarter. Now if a woman in the rain became worried about her makeup, she had only to raise the umbrella high enough to flip open the cap and take a look at herself. But even this was not enough for Sam Foster. He had personally observed many times that one of the public problems caused by women was their inability to locate a nickel in the bottom of their purse to pay their fare on a crowded streetcar during the rush hour. Sam wanted to put an end to this familiar traffic jam. He had an indentation made in the base of the handle itself, just big enough to hold a nickel. Now a woman in the rain, waiting for a streetcar, could, having checked her makeup in the mirror, board the car, close the umbrella, flip the cap again, extract her nickel, pay her fare, enter the car, and maybe get a seat, and the world could go on. It was a great idea, but the fact of life that ruined it was the fact that life was getting a little more expensive. Carfare went up to seven cents. This presented an engineering problem that even Sam Foster couldn't resolve—and nobody else did since. The familiar traffic jam remained a public problem.

Enterprise, successful or not, seemed to be a Foster family trait, and Joe Foster gave evidence of it at an early age. Throughout his boyhood, Joe Foster was on a modest allowance, and if he ran short any week, he was expected to earn what he needed at any odd jobs he could find. He was not allowed to turn to the Foster Grant Company, Inc., because of what might be considered an unfair advantage over other young job-seekers, in view of his relationship to the President. One summer while he was in high school, however, Joe came to the conclusion that his contact at Foster Grant was too good to pass up entirely. He talked about this to a friend, Sam Rapaporte, suggesting, "Why don't we get a carload of my father's products and try selling them door-to-door? We could make a fortune." This sounded like a good idea to Sam Rapaporte. It sounded like an interesting idea to Sam Foster.

But Sam Foster asked, "Where would you sell? You wouldn't have any luck in Leominster."

"I suppose you're right," Joe conceded. "We'll go somewhere else."

"Where?"

"Binghamton, New York."

"Why Binghamton?"

"I don't know. I just thought of it. It sounds like a good town."

"All right. Binghamton, then."

They left Leominster on a Monday morning in a borrowed car, the back of it crammed with Sam's own products, which he had advanced to them on consignment at the same wholesale price he gave everybody else. They arrived in Binghamton in the late afternoon, just in time to check into the Y.M.C.A. and call it a day. Next morning, they drove out to a residential section and began, block after block after block, working opposite sides of the street. By late afternoon, they both had sore feet from walking, sore jaws from talking, sore arms from carrying the heavy display cases, and they had not sold a thing. They called it a day.

Wednesday passed the same, with one exception. A woman asked Joe, "Do you have a city license to peddle?"

"No, I don't," Joe admitted.

"Then you'd better get one," she said. "You're breaking the law."

Joe crossed the street to Sam Rapaporte and gave him the news. Sam said, "Maybe we'd better get one. What do you think it would cost?"

Joe said, "What's the difference? At the rate we've been going, a license would be a bad investment at any price."

"What do you want to do, then?"

"Let's risk it," Joe said. It wasn't much of a risk. They ended the day without a sale. And Thursday was the same. Thursday evening, Joe asked, "Had enough, Sam?"

Sam said, "I had enough Tuesday."

"Then let's go home tomorrow."

"Good."

Joe said, "I just hate going home without making a single sale. My father will think there's something wrong with his products."

Sam suggested, "Why don't we throw the stuff away?"

"What'll we use to pay for it?"

They almost did throw it away. Heading home, Joe got an idea. A slight detour took them into the resort hotel area of the Catskill Mountains. They went from hotel to hotel and practically gave the products away to the people who operated concessions in the hotels, but at least they got rid of it. They got enough to pay Sam Foster, and all they were out were their travel expenses and their dreams of early wealth.

Perhaps it was this experience that dissuaded Joe Foster from seriously considering going into business with his father. Instead, Joe chose law. After finishing at the Leominster high school, he attended Williston Academy and then entered Boston University for pre-law.

Meanwhile, Sam Foster came upon what he considered a good opportunity to buy some equipment. Despite the work slow-down that hit Leominster in 1921 after Irene Castle cut her hair, Foster Grant was doing well. Sam had his bird cages and costume jewelry, and the Goodmans were giving him a lot of work. Though women stopped buying the large combs they used to hold their long hair in place when they wore it up, they still needed hairpins, barrettes, combs, brushes, and curlers. The equipment Sam heard about was in a factory in Providence, the owner of which had died. The man's family chose not to carry on the business, and the executor advertised an auction in the New England papers. Sam Foster and Fred England went to Providence to examine the machinery, and they agreed that it was in good shape. The sealed bid they entered was, they felt, generous, and it turned out to be far more generous than they thought. They not only acquired the machinery; they acquired a going concern, including the building, the stock, the staff, and a backlog of orders.

England asked, "What do we do now, Sam?"

Sam said, "I don't know. We can't just move out the

machinery and forget the rest of it. We'll have to find somebody to run it."

This was in 1924. One weekend, Joe, then twenty-one, came home from college, and Sam greeted him with: "Joe, do you want to be a lawyer, or do you want to get married?"

Joe said, "I want to get married."

Sam said, "Then go to work."

Thus Joseph Foster began his career in business, working for his father, after all, and Foster Grant got an heir. One day, Sam Foster was to say to Abe Goodman, "Abe, that son I've got is a diamond. A real diamond."

3

There were oldtimers at Foster Grant during the Golden Anniversary Year who could remember the day Joseph Foster came to work with the company, and they remark on his talent for management from the start. In the early days, management was a matter Sam Foster carried around in his head. He handled events as they came up, dismissing them once they were resolved. He disliked paperwork and he kept no records. Taxes were a simpler matter in those days, and Sam left his to the woman who made out his payroll. Joe

Foster brought a sense of organization to the company. His mind, keyed for law, was keyed for orderliness and system. Sam Foster saw the company as a finely tuned instrument that could turn out excellent workmanship. Joe Foster saw the company as a living entity which would have to grow and expand steadily in order to survive. And yet the two views blended perfectly. He has built an empire.

❋ ❋ ❋ ❋

Going to work as the manager of the Providence factory did not make Joe Foster immediately solvent, and so he did not marry for another four years. But he already had the girl in mind: Esther Winthrop, who lived in Fitchburg, five miles from Leominster. They had met while they were in high school, dated, and they continued to date into their college years. They knew they would one day marry, but because of what they expected would be Joe's six years of study for his law degree, they knew they would have to wait. Now that Joe was a working man, they knew they would have to wait only until he was solvent. As a step in that direction, Joe lived inexpensively at the Broad Street Y.M.C.A. in Providence. As another step, he made a point of visiting his Providence uncles and aunts around mealtime.

Joe remained at Providence about a year. By then, Fred England was again considering retirement, and he took steps to dissolve his partnership with Sam Foster. By then, too, Sam Foster realized that his Manning Avenue and Spruce Street facilities were too small. On Lancaster Street, he located a three-building compound with a combined floor space of forty thousand square feet, and he began to negotiate for it. Meanwhile, Sam instructed Joe to start phasing out the Providence jewelry operation. Joe thought this meant he would be returning to Leominster and to Esther, but Sam had other plans for him.

Confident of company growth, Sam Foster was taking on extra help at a time when a business slump in Leominster made extra help plentiful. One new employee at this time was Conrad LeBlanc, then a teenager. One morning as he was about to leave for school, his brother, who already worked for Sam, came running home from work, and he asked, "Connie, do you want a job?"

Connie said, "Sure."

"Sam Foster needs somebody today."

"Just for today?"

"I don't know."

"I don't care." Connie put down his books, picked up his lunch box, and then hurried with his brother to the Manning Avenue plant. At the time of Foster Grant's Golden Anniversary, Conrad LeBlanc had been with the company forty-three years and was heading the Design and Development Section of the sunglasses division. During the intervening years, Conrad found among the Foster Grant employees the girl he eventually married. On the company records in Conrad LeBlanc's name were several patents which practically revolutionized sunglass manufacture.

Another newcomer during this transition period was Bernard (Bunny) McDowell, who made his way to Foster Grant one morning on a sad and familiar pursuit in Leominster: a job. Entering the office, he asked Sam's secretary, Alice, "Do you people have any openings?"

Alice said, "See Sam Foster. He's in the plant."

There was an opening, at Spruce Street, assembling the bird cages, and after Sam hired McDowell, Bunny said thanks, turned, and headed for the door and Spruce Street. Sam called, "Wait a minute. Don't you want to know what the job pays?"

Bunny said, "I'm so glad to have a job that I don't care what it pays."

Ten years later, Bunny McDowell made his job even more secure than it was by marrying the boss's secretary. Alice McDowell was retired by the time of the Golden Anniversary, but Bunny, then in his forty-first year with the company, had worked at just about every job in the plant and held a high management position. There were many others still on the payroll whose lives had followed a similar pattern.

By the beginning of 1927, most of the Foster Grant facilities were settled at Lancaster Street. Manning Avenue was closed; Spruce Street was phasing out; in Providence, Joe Foster was shipping the last of the machinery to Leominster before shutting down the building and heading home himself. He expected that Sam would give him some managerial assignment in the office while supervising the production himself. But Joe had no sooner made himself comfortable at home than one night Sam said, "Joe, I want you to go to New York."

Joe said, "Okay, Dad. What for?"

Sam said, "We should have somebody there handling the sales of our own articles."

"You want me to hire somebody?" Joe asked.

"I want you to do the selling," Sam said. "That's your new job."

Joe's heart sank. New York was farther away than Providence, which would put him farther away from Esther Winthrop. He tested. "You expect me to *live* in New York, Dad?"

"You expect to *commute* every day?" Sam returned. "I didn't know you loved your home so much." And he smiled.

Joe moved to New York. He has recalled, "For twenty-five dollars a month, I was able to rent a desk and a chair, get a phone and a place to hang my hat. I was able to get our regular customers to buy a little more and to find a few new customers to buy a little. It wasn't as bad as Binghamton."

On the contrary, it was wonderful. Joe Foster put his father's company into the big time this way: Sam came up with an idea for a small memo pad. When Joe Foster received a sample from Leominster, he studied it, wondering where to take it. At the time, Foster Grant was selling its own articles only to jobbers and wholesalers, and ever since he had arrived in New York, Joe had been aching for some way to get into the chain variety stores—the big time, indeed. Could this be it?

Joe called the Woolworth office and got an appointment with a buyer by the name of Hockinson. Next day, sitting opposite the man in the Woolworth office, Joe handed him the pad and asked, "What do you think of this, sir?"

Hockinson examined it. "A memo pad?"

"Yes, sir. It's the sort of thing a woman would carry in her purse."

"Yes," said the buyer, studying, thinking. "Very clever. Attractive. How much do you want for it?"

Joe cleared his throat, nervous, hopeful. "We figure it as a ten-cent item. You can have it for seventy-five cents a dozen, nine dollars a gross."

The man nodded. "Ought to have a pencil, though."

Joe leaned forward. "I beg your pardon?"

"A pencil. The thing ought to have a pencil attached to it. That would make it even more convenient."

"A pencil," Joe said, not sure.

"Yes. Have you ever seen those dance cards that women use at formal parties?"

"Yes, sir."

"They have a pencil attached. A little pencil. On a string."

"Yes, sir."

Hockinson passed the pad back to Joe. "You put a pencil on that and you'll really have something."

Joe said, "Yes, sir. But we don't make pencils."

"Hell, man, other people do!" The buyer's impatience worried Joe a bit. Then the man calmed. "The American Pencil Company is right down the street. Why don't you go and see them? You figure out a way to put a pencil on this thing and I'll give you an order."

Joe said, "Thank you, sir. I'll be back."

He went directly to the American Pencil Company, where he told the clerk, "I want to see some pencils, please. Small pencils. Little enough to be attached to this." He held up the memo pad.

The clerk asked, "You want to attach a pencil to that?"

"Yes."

"Do you mind if I ask why?"

Joe explained, "I work for the Foster Grant Company, in Leominster, Massachusetts—"

"Where?"

"In Massachusetts. We make the pad. Now we've decided to attach a pencil to it. I'm looking for the right kind of pencil. It has to be little."

The clerk shook his head. "Let me see if I've got this straight. You want me to sell you some pencils you can attach to your pads and then sell to other people?"

"That's right."

"I don't know if I can do that," the clerk said. "I'll have to check with the boss."

Joe said, "Before you bother the boss, let's see if you have the pencils I want." The clerk brought an assortment and Joe chose the one he felt was right, and he asked, "How much are these by the gross?"

"Two dollars a gross."

"About a penny and a half each."

"Yes."

That would be tight. The pad was selling at 6.5 cents each by the dozen, 6.25 cents by the gross, and nothing could be added to that if Woolworth was to make any money selling them for a dime. The cost of the pencil, then, would have to be absorbed by Foster Grant, probably cutting the company's profit in half. Joe asked, "Can I get them for less if I buy them in large quantities?"

"That's what I'll have to ask the boss," the clerk said, and he headed down a corridor. He was back in a moment, shaking his head again, and he said, "The boss said no. We're not in the wholesale business."

"I'll take a gross, anyway," Joe said. "I'll let you know if I need more."

Joe went back to his desk and telephoned Sam, and he said, "Dad, I'm close to selling the memo pad to Woolworth."

Sam said, "That's wonderful, Joe. How many do they want?"

"They haven't decided, Dad. They want us to make a change."

"A change?"

"They want us to attach a pencil to it."

"A pencil?"

"Yes. It would be a great convenience. I think it's a good idea, Dad."

"Of course it is. We should have thought of it ourselves," Sam said. "Now, where do we get the pencils?"

"I've found some," Joe said. Then, "Dad, I think I ought to come home about this. It could be big."

"Come home, Joe."

Next day, they were standing together in Sam's office and Sam was studying the pad and the pencil. He said, "But a cent and a half apiece, Joe. Do you know what that does to the mark-up?"

"Yes."

"How did the buyer say the pencil should be attached?"

"He suggested a string."

"Then we'd have to buy the string. There would go everything."

"I know."

Sam said, "Joe, I know Woolworth is important, but do you think you could sell the pad as it is to somebody else?"

Joe said, "If I could sell it to Woolworth, I could sell it to everybody else. That's why I went there first."

"I know." Still studying the pad and pencil, Sam brought the pencil up against the edge of the pad and held it there. "Come on," he said, and he led Joe into the shop, to a scrap barrel. He chose a discarded chip of plastic and took it to a man at a workbench. Sam said, "Carl, I want you to try something for me. Soften this up and thin it out a bit; then see if you can make a small tube, just big enough to hold this little pencil."

Sam and Joe stood at the man's side for the few minutes it took to make the tube and insert the pencil. Perfect fit. Sam placed the inserted pencil at the side of the pad and said: "Now all we need is some glue and Mr. Woolworth will have his memo pad." Joe Foster stared at his father in amazement, and Sam caught this. Sam smiled. He said, "You know what I like best, Joe? We can use the scraps. We can cut down on waste." He extracted the pencil and looked unhappily at it and said, "Now, if I could just find some way out of buying these things."

Out of his amazement, Joe suggested, "Why don't you go back to the scrap barrel?" It was more of a tease.

But Sam looked at Joe in amazement, and said, "You've got something there, Joe. We can molt the scraps down, add a coloring, and then let it harden into little crayons."

"Can that be done?"

"We can give it a try."

"How soon will you know?"

"I can put somebody on it right away. Why?"

"I would like to get a sample back to New York fast, while Mr. Woolworth is still interested."

Two days later, Woolworth's buyer was inspecting a sample at his desk, and he said, "Well, this came out very nice. Is the price the same?"

"Yes, sir," said Joe. "Seventy-five cents a dozen and nine dollars a gross."

"All right. I'll take three thousand."

Joe began to write out the order, saying, "Three . . . thousand . . . memo pads, number . . ."

The buyer said, "No. That's three thousand *gross*."

Joe's hand shook. It was an order for over twenty-five thousand dollars, the biggest single order for any Foster Grant article. Joe Foster went from the Woolworth office across town to another variety chain and announced, "I've just sold this to Woolworth." Before the week was out, he sold two and a half million of the pads. Over the next few years, tens of millions were sold, not only through stores but as give-away souvenirs by businesses of all kinds. It was at Foster Grant that the technique for imprinting "commercials" on the plastic substance was devised. In time, the pads were made in different sizes and various colors, the covers decorated sometimes with rhinestones or chips of colored glass, sometimes with plastic flowers or a mirror or an initial or even a compass. And the Woolworth necessity proved to be the mother of another invention for several years Foster Grant put out a successful line of plastic crayons.

The country began to open up for Foster Grant, and so did the world. It was soon obvious that there was more territory than Joe Foster could cover alone. Hired to work with him was William Rubin, who had been a partner in the Imperial Novelty Company, of New York, which had been buying its blanks—undecorated articles—from Foster Grant for a few years. While Joe Foster focused his efforts along the East Coast, Rubin covered the rest of the country, occasionally accompanied by Joe. At the end of one of their joint trips, Joe Foster had an experience that definitely overcame any doubts he might have had about the career in which he seemed settled for life.

They parted in Detroit, Rubin heading west, Joe boarding the "Wolverine" for his return east. When Joe went into the dining car for dinner, he was seated opposite an older man whose affluence was evident in his clothes, his jewelry, and his manner. Joe felt a little out of place. They started chatting.

The man asked, "What business are you in?"

Joe said, "I'm a salesman."

"For whom?"

"Foster Grant."

"What do they make?"

"Novelties."

"What kind of novelties?"

Joe shrugged. "Just nickel-and-dime stuff."

The man leaned forward and looked Joe squarely in the eyes, and he said: "Young man, don't dismiss nickel-and-dime stuff as unimportant just because it sounds cheap. Never forget the empire Mr. Wrigley has built on his nickel chewing gum."

Joe Foster never forgot, and he also never forgot the

underlying axiom in the man's analogy: "You don't have to be ashamed of the price of your product as long as you can be proud of its quality. Soon Joe was leaning forward and excitedly telling the man about the memo pads.

Changes were happening fast.

This happened: Foster Grant began doing business in Mexico. The first customer was Shriber & Company, an American firm distributing hair ornaments in Mexico. Latin women had evidently been unimpressed by Irene Castle's haircut and were still wearing their hair long. Thus, as Foster Grant was getting its roots in its new home on Lancaster Street, the company found itself again making large, decorated combs for Mexico.

Another American firm doing business in Mexico and which became a Foster Grant customer was the Harry Bergman Company, with Harry Bergman himself directing operations there. After establishing his company well enough so that it did not require his firsthand supervision, Bergman returned to the United States. He remained in New York briefly, then settled in Leominster, working out of the Foster Grant facilities. Besides being a good customer, Harry Bergman picked up the Foster Grant surplus at the end of the season, thus allowing the company to clear out its inventory.

Harry Bergman also did business with European companies, and on one of his trips to Germany he had met Rudolph Riesenfeld, who, though a teen-ager, was already at work for an exporter. Bergman was at Leominster when he received a letter from Rudolph in which the boy, then seventeen, expressed his apprehensions about a rising political figure by the name of Adolf Hitler. Rudy said, "I don't know what Hitler's plans for Germany are, but I expect the worst. If there is any way you can help me get out of this country, I will be grateful." Bergman brought the young man to Leominster, where he worked both for Foster Grant and for the Bergman company, handling Bergman's paper work when he went on the road, as he was now free to do.

One day Harry Bergman asked Sam Foster, "Have you ever thought of opening a plant in Mexico?"

Sam said, "No, I haven't."

"You should, Sam," Bergman suggested. "You'd do very well down there. No competition, really, not in your class. All the good stuff still comes from outside the country."

"It would cost a lot of money."

"Just at first," said Bergman. "But think of what you'd save in freight. And think of this: the cost of living is much lower than in the United States. You could be selling at the same prices, but your production costs would be a fraction of what they are here."

"It's something to think about," Sam conceded.

It was the sort of thing Sam Foster enjoyed thinking about. He was approaching fifty, an age when most men would be content to have one successful business to their credit, but his interest in life, in change, in challenge, was as lively as ever, and Sam Foster was not the kind of man who would think that the time had come for him to settle down. In the years ahead, Sam would start more than one new life.

And this had happened: In August, 1929, Abe Goodman decided to spend a week or so on vacation at Grossinger's, the famous resort hotel in the Catskills. Before heading for the mountains, Abe called Joe Foster, to let him know where he would be, and he said, "Joe, you've been working too hard. You could use a vacation yourself. Why don't you come up and spend a few days with me at Grossinger's? The rest would do you good, and I'd enjoy having you be my guest."

Joe said, "All right, Abe. That sounds good to me. I'll be there next Wednesday."

That Wednesday, Abe Goodman and Joe Foster were alone in a rowboat on the lake at Grossinger's. The lake was quiet, with just two or three other rowboats in the distance. Joe could sense that Abe Goodman had something on his mind; he had an idea what it was.

"You know, Joe," Abe Goodman began, "my brother and I have always enjoyed working with your father."

"Dad has enjoyed it, too, I know," said Joe. "You're our best customers."

"I don't mean just that way," said Abe, with a slight frown. "I mean personally. We are all good friends. We are like one family. We are as close as brothers with Sam."

"That's true. Dad feels the same way. He has said so many times."

"Good. And you, Joe?"

"I feel the same."

"Good. Joe, your father is doing very well; he may want to retire some day; you will take over the company, of course, and—"

Joe had to laugh. "Dad will never quit working."

"You never know," said Abe. "Anyway, Joe, lately Jack and I have been thinking about something that I'd like to mention to you. Do you think your father would be interested in having us on a partnership basis in Foster Grant?"

Joe's hunch was right. He knew, too, that the idea had already occurred to Sam, but he could not speak for Sam now. He said, "I'll talk to Dad about it."

"Good."

They left it at that.

The following week, back in his office, Abe Goodman had several matters to discuss with Sam Foster and therefore telephoned him. They talked about the other matters. Finally, Abe Goodman asked, "Sam, has Joe mentioned what I talked to him about at Grossinger's?"

"The partnership?"

"Yes."

"Yes, Abe. Joe mentioned it."

"How do you feel about it, Sam?"

"I like it, Abe. I think it is fine. It would be good for all of us."

"I'm glad to hear that, Sam. Sam, how much would be involved for us?"

"I don't know, Abe. I haven't thought about that part."

"Mention a figure, Sam."

"It would be a full partnership, wouldn't it?"

"We would like that."

"All right, Abe. Fifty thousand dollars?"

"All right, Sam. I'll send you a check."

That's all there was to it. No lawyers. No negotiations. No contract. Just a friendly chat on the phone.

Like most businessmen of that time, Abe and Jack Goodman were investing in the stock market. Now in search of a convenient fifty thousand dollars, they examined their portfolio. For a few years, they'd had holdings in the American Power and Light Company, and their broker now told them that they could sell what they had for fifty thousand dollars and change. They sold it. In a week or so, their check was on its way to Leominster. Sam Foster endorsed the check and banked it, and with that he got himself a pair of partners. There was no discussion as to who would be president or how policy would be determined or anything like that. It was assumed that Sam would continue to run the company, that one day Joe would take over, and all the Goodmans expected was that they would be consulted in the event of any important moves that might require a sizable investment.

Within a week after the Goodmans' check cleared their own bank, the stock market crashed. In a single afternoon, the fifty thousand dollars the Goodmans had had in American Power and Light wasn't worth a dime. Thus by the series of fortunate coincidences the Goodmans were not only saved from a painful financial loss, but they acquired the partnership literally for free.

In 1929, the future of Foster Grant looked good. Nobody realized how good it was going to be.

❊ ❊ ❊ ❊

Nobody who knew Sam Foster at the time could later remember why he decided to start making sunglasses. Nobody could remember exactly when the first sunglasses were made. The company was at Lancaster Street then, so it probably was between 1927 and 1929. But people remember this: the design for the first Foster Grant sunglasses was sketched on a piece of ordinary brown wrapping paper. The paper was moistened in oil and applied to a piece of plastic the size of the frame. This piece was placed on a pile of four or five more pieces, all of them gripped together by metal clamps. Then somebody, using a jigsaw, cut out the first Foster Grant frames. The temple bars were made in the same crude fashion. The first Foster Grant sunglasses sold for ten cents a pair and were marketed as a kiddie item—a toy.

Around this time, there were a number of optical companies in the country manufacturing spectacles for improved vision. Usually glasses were rimless, with metal temples. Metal frames had a period of popularity, as did horn and shell. The use of plastics for frames and temples was just beginning in the late Twenties, which therefore placed Foster Grant among the pioneers, probably the pioneer, using plastics for sunglasses.

There were at the time perhaps four or five American companies making sunglasses, and the glasses were not a quantity item. Other glasses were coming in from abroad, but also in limited amounts. Sunglasses simply had not caught on as yet, either as a utilitarian or a fashion item, and what Sam Foster foresaw in them as a commercial product can only be attributed to his own business acumen.

People have been seeking eye protection from glare ever since the first man was forced to squint. It is now known that for centuries Eskimos, though isolated from world trends, chiseled slits in mollusk half-shells and attached them to

SAMUEL FOSTER, JR., 1883–1966. Founder and First President Foster Grant Co., Inc.

AN OLD TUNE: The former Richardson Piano Factory—now Foster Grant Co., in Leominster, as seen half a century ago.

KEY MACHINE: In 1930, Sam Foster brought over from Germany a new machine for injection molding of plastics. Foster Grant technicians made the machine commercially adaptable, permitting Foster Grant to become the first American company to adopt injection molding.

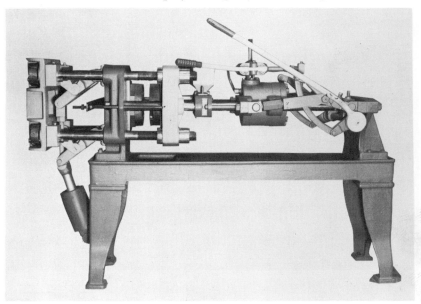

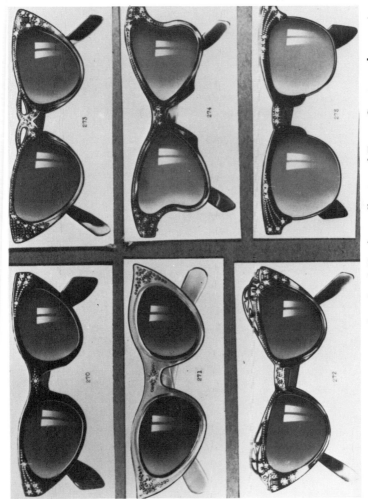

SHADES OF THE PAST: Remember these? Here's a collection of Foster Grant sunglasses, vintage 1940. Even then, Foster Grant was the world's largest sunglass manufacturer.

LET 'ER GO!: Joe Foster, sunglasses in hand, turns on production at Foster
Grant's monostyrene plant in Baton Rouge, La. The year: 1954.

NUMBER ONE: The first of Foster Grant's own tank cars to arrive at Leominster from Baton Rouge, La. in the early 1950's.

Governor John Volpe of Massachusetts (left) and screen star Carroll Baker joined Joe Foster at the 1966 dedication of the Samuel Foster Sunglass Plant in Leominster, the most modern production facility in the sunglass industry. Miss Baker was then starring in Foster Grant's "Sunglasses of the Stars" advertising campaign.

A TOAST: Joe Foster (left) is toasted by Robert Siegfried, president of The Badger Company, Inc., during the 1969 groundbreaking ceremonies on the big new addition to the Foster Grant monostyrene production facility at Baton Rouge, La. Badger, one of the world's largest engineering and construction firms, built the plant addition.

BIG DAY: Joe Foster, joined by several Foster Grant directors and company officers, addresses a throng at the 1969 dedication of the Baton Rouge monostyrene plant.

Isn't that Raquel Welch
behind those Foster Grants?

(Yes indeed. See her in "Bandolero," from 20th Century Fox.)

To remove any further speculation, we'll own up. That is Miss Welch.

But, as you can see, our Foster Grants (known to many as the Sunglasses of the Stars) have done it again. They've given Raquel a new dimension. Several in fact.

One moment she's capricious. Then contented. Now candid. Even coy.

That, kind heart, is the Spell of the Shades.

Long, long ago folks wore sunglasses only when they were under the sun. Now they wear them from sun up till sun up. From New Year's Day till New Year's Eve.

In every kind of weather. Everywhere.

Sunglasses have become funglasses.

We can't tell you how happy that makes us, since Foster Grant is clearly the leader in the anti-glare business.

We have more styles in more colors than anybody.

And they all have ff77 lenses that meet U.S. Government standards for eye protection (standards a lot of expensive imports don't meet).

Now, if somebody mentioned sunglasses, who would you think of first?

Besides Raquel Welch.

"So you admit you didn't come to Zermatt just to climb the Matterhorn."

"Am I doomed, C. B., to play the sex symbol in an age of flower children?"

"... and now, love, you know all my secrets."

"If you really wanted to hang on to Rhodesia, Sir Robert, why didn't you tell me?"

"Any man who straightens his tie as often as you just has to be hiding something."

"Matador, you're looking at a w who wants more than a moment o

VIVA RAQUEL!: The Raquel Welch advertisement for Foster Grant sunglasses, which appeare in *Life* Magazine, among other publications, was judged one of the best-read ads of 1968. An small wonder.

headbands of leather thongs, in this way cutting down the glare of the sun on snow while hunting or fighting. In the tropics, people evidently have always cut small holes in broad leaves which they tied around their heads. People have used colored glass for eye protection ever since they found out how to make colored glass. In the ancient Orient, men and women wore face masks made of tiny beads on strings. During the Roman Era, abrasives were used to make precious stones smooth enough and thin enough to be placed in something like a lorgnette. A similar article was used by the rich during the Renaissance, but in an ostentatious show of affluence. Tinted protective glasses were used a hundred years ago in industry, by men who worked at open furnaces or at welding.

Sunglasses for general use might never have caught on if the motion picture industry had not moved to sunny Hollywood. Affluent movie stars had sunglasses made for themselves, and when pictures of them wearing sunglasses started appearing in the fan magazines, it was probably inevitable that a new fad was on the way. Sam Foster wasn't much of a movie fan and probably never looked at a fan magazine, but someone's chance comment about this trend would have been all that Sam needed to start his mind off on another idea. In any event, Sam Foster was undoubtedly the first manufacturer in the world to think of sunglasses as a mass-appeal item, and from the start he aimed in that direction.

In the administration building of Foster Grant at Leominster, there is a massive switchboard which requires the full-time services of four operators. Most of the calls are long distance, going and coming. Many of them are overseas

55

calls. The Foster Grant outreach into the world of international business was a natural progression for an ambitious company. Even before World War II, when Foster Grant had still to achieve its first one million dollar year, the company was already involved in joint ventures and partnerships with foreign manufacturers. Later on, when Foster Grant went into plastics, the foreign field offered the best routs, particularly in the area of ideas.

At the time, the plastics industry in America was dominated by three or four giants who had the money—or could get it—to build the huge and complicated facilities they thought necessary for production. It was commonly held that the only way you could operate profitably was to produce in enormous quantities. Joseph Foster felt differently. He believed that a well-managed small producer could compete successfully against much larger competitors.

Experience had taught Joe Foster that many European manufacturers operated on the same principle he did. There were, of course, some huge companies in Europe, but most of them were smaller manufacturers who, facing severe competition from similar manufacturers in other European countries, had to depend primarily on the local market and therefore geared themselves to limited production. It was a matter of doing big things in a small way. Thus, when Joe Foster decided the time had come to lead Foster Grant into the production of plastics, he knew what he wanted to do and he knew where to look to find out whether it could be done. He was able to proceed on familiar grounds because of the experience the company already had had with foreign ventures.

First, there had been Mexico.

4

Early in 1930, Sam Foster conceded that Harry Bergman had a good idea. It was worth looking into. But because
of the size of the venture, Sam felt the initial step should be
a first-hand inspection of the potentials—a trip to Mexico.
He and Bergman left New York on a luxury liner which took
them to Merida, on the Yucatan coast, and here they transferred to a coastal freighter which took them to Veracruz.
After a week in Veracruz, they obtained a car and began to
zigzag their way northward, searching for the best location.
They decided on Monterrey. It was then the most im-

portant industrial city in Mexico, with a large population that was factory-oriented, excellent utilities, and good natural resources. The mayor had been profuse in his offer of co-operation. The fact that Monterrey was just one hundred and fifty miles into Mexico from Laredo, Texas, struck Sam as an economic advantage in terms of bringing in the plastics he would need from U.S. companies. The fact that there was nothing between the two cities except a dirt road cutting through one hundred and fifty miles of wasteland did not bother him. When he returned to Leominster, Sam was on fire to get going. Others, including Joe Foster, were not as enthusiastic. They saw certain obstacles.

In the first place, though the mayor of Monterrey was ready to grant tax concessions, there was no building for the new project. A factory would have to be built. This would be expensive; and the quality of the construction work was questionable. In the second place, most of Northern Mexico was still guerrilla territory for gangs of bandits left over from the Pancho Villa days, and there was no guarantee that anything that left Laredo would ever reach Monterrey.

Sam was good-naturedly adamant. He felt he had already solved the factory problem. He would have the building designed by American architects, according to his personal specifications, and would put the structure to a test by actually having it pieced together in Leominster before dismantling it and shipping by sea to Veracruz and then by land to Monterrey. Equipment would be shipped the same way. As for the bandits, Sam had had no trouble with them on his own trip through Mexico and he considered them an exaggerated threat.

Near the end of 1930, the factory building, surely one of the world's first prefabs, was on its way to Monterrey. So was the equipment. Sam wanted to find out for himself about the bandits. With two friends, he left Leominster by car one morning and drove safely into Monterrey five days later. The only trouble they had occurred in Texas. A sudden rainstorm forced them off the road and into a gully; and they lost a few hours looking for a tow truck to pull them out. Three months later, Sam Foster was back in Leominster, the Mexican operation a going concern. It was called the National Pyralart Company, a name concocted by Joe from (a) Pyraveer, the plastic to be used there, and (b) the fact that the company would be making objects of art.

Sam was very pleased with the way the project had begun and was confident of the future. Harry Bergman had agreed to remain in Mexico to supervise the factory and direct the sales force. Rudy Riesenfeld was in Mexico, too, as Bergman's assistant. On parting with them, Sam had said, "I know the plant will be in good hands, so I don't expect to do any worrying. But if anything goes wrong, call me at Leominster at any time of the day or night. And if you need me, I'll get here as fast as I can."

The next time Sam Foster went to Mexico, he became involved in a venture that was climaxed by kidnapping and murder.

* * * *

Sam took to Lancaster Street his Manning Avenue mania for constantly rearranging a room to get more space. He felt that if he could get one more foot out of a room, the extra work of rearranging the place was worth it; and even when he got the foot, it would be only a couple of weeks before Sam would walk into the room, look around unhappily, and say, "We ought to be able to get more space out of this shop. If any of you want to make some overtime, I could use your help Saturday afternoon." Overtime had its appeal, of course, but the men were familiar with this trait in Sam and they thought it was fun, and so they were willing to put in the extra hours just to see how Sam was going to manage to get one more inch out of a room. Somehow Sam always managed. Sometimes he managed something else: shoved behind a machine or a workbench or at the back of a stockroom would be a box of valuable inventory that nobody knew was there. So the rearranging went on and on at Lancaster Street. It could be hard work. Some of the machines were very heavy. One Saturday, after hours of huffing and puffing and moaning and groaning, one man asked, "Hey, Sam, wouldn't it be easier on all of us around here if we just put everything on wheels?" Everything that could be put on wheels was put on wheels. And the rearranging went on and on.

There was one area, however, where Sam would tolerate waste, and this was for the sake of quality. And Sam wanted his men to share this concern with him. Sam would stroll through a workshop, stop at a worker's side, inspect his output, then frown to himself if the work was slipshod. Rather than criticize the man, Sam would ask amiably, "How are these things coming out?" If the man said he thought the items were coming out all right, Sam would just nod and move on. Before leaving the shop, however, Sam would tell the foreman to see to it that the man's work was put aside as rejects. And that was the last time the easily satisfied worker was put on anything except routine production, shutting the door on himself to promotions and raises. On the other hand, a worker who knew Sam and felt close to him, which was practically every man who worked for Sam for any length of time, would more likely say, "To tell you the truth, Sam, I'm getting disgusted. I don't know if it's the machine or this batch of plastics or me, but I haven't been able to turn out one decent piece all morning. I'm ready to junk this stuff and take the day off and go fishing." Sam would laugh and say, "Listen, everybody has a bad day once in a while. Yes, let's junk this stuff. I'm not proud of it, either. Now, if you want to go to another machine, go to another machine, but if you'd rather go fishing, go fishing." And Sam would gladly pay the man for his day's efforts, however he decided to spend the rest of it.

And it was the same way with the sunglasses. For the first year or so, more of the Foster Grant production ended up in the scrap barrel than went out on the market. Sam's demand for quality was responsible for this to some extent, but there were other reasons. The chemical industry had not as yet ironed out all the wrinkles in the production of plastics, nor were there machines which could make the best commercial use of the plastics then available. On going into the sunglass business, Foster Grant was the victim of both these circumstances; and in order to stay in the sunglass business, the people at Foster Grant went ahead and did what they had always done when confronted with problems. They solved the problems themselves.

The first Foster Grant sunglasses were handmade because there was no other way. One man spent all day jigsawing frames from sheets of plastic. Another spent all day gouging a groove on the inner side of each eye section. Another man softened the frames with heat, allowing the next man to snap the glass lenses into the grooves. A lot of lenses got broken. So Sam suggested, "Is there a way we can make the frames with an open side so that the lenses can be placed into position and then somehow sealed in?" There was a way. The frames were cut with a collar in the back. The lenses would be placed into position in warmed frames; then a metal plunger would be lowered to fold the collar over the glass. A lot of lenses were still being broken, but not as many as before. Years would pass before this problem was finally solved. The glass was part of the problem. The glass, tinted to the required color by the glass manufacturer, was delivered in sheets and then cut to the proper sizes and shapes at Foster Grant. Rarely did two sheets of glass have exactly the same thickness, and it was this inconsistency that made it difficult to design a machine which could fold the collar over without breaking those lenses that were too thick.

And the plastics were part of the problem, too. If a plastics producer had trouble with his machinery or turned out a bad batch, its customers paid for it through late deliveries or unusable material. It was Joe Foster who first suggested that Foster Grant should produce its own plastics. At that time, the Tennessee Eastman Company had begun to produce cellulose acetate in the form of flakes. Joe thought it would be a good idea for Foster Grant to obtain the flakes and do its own plasticizing. In this way, his company could better control quality and have a sure source of supply. As simple as this seems, it was also revolutionary. Around 1930, the giant chemical companies zealously protected their trade secrets and markets. The idea was so unusual that Tennessee Eastman didn't know what to make of it when Joe Foster first broached the subject of buying its flakes. It looked as though Eastman were being asked to go into competition with itself. But Joe Foster stressed that his company did not intend to market the acetate, but only to use it to make consumer products. In time, other chemical companies, including those owning manufacturing outlets, decided this was all right, too. Thus Foster Grant took its first step into the manufacture of plastic materials, a field that was to contribute phenomenally to the company's growth. Before that growth could begin, however, there was another problem to be solved, and it was the biggest problem of all.

❊   ❊   ❊   ❊

Many people had the wrong idea about plastics. They thought that a plastic was a substitute for a natural substance and therefore not as good. To these people, anything plastic was a cheap imitation. This was, of course, a ridiculous notion, evolving mostly from a lack of information, but it lingered a long time.

The word plastic is derived from the Greek *plastikos*, meaning "to form," and plastics are materials, natural or synthetic, that are capable of being formed into usable products by heating, milling, molding, and similar processes.

"Synthetic" is a word with a bad reputation of its own. To some people, a synthetic is something artificial, something spurious, something that is not what it seems to be. Synthesis is the assembling of separate or subordinate parts into a new form. In chemistry, it is the building up of compounds in a series of reactions involving elements, radicals, or simpler compounds; and the chemist ends up with a material which often is identical to a naturally occurring substance, and it is generally as good and usually better than the natural substance.

Another word for plastic materials is "resins," and here is another tricky word. Before the advent of synthetic resins, the term "resin" was applied only to certain sticky substances which exude in the form of yellow or brown deposits from certain trees, such as the pine and the fir. The substance appears when the bark of the tree is injured, as by wind, fire, lightning, or commercial tapping. After being exposed to the air for a short time, the substance hardened, and in this form it was a very durable substance. Archeologists have found underground deposits of resins in places where trees haven't grown for thousands of years.

The people of ancient times found uses for resins. They observed that resin melted when heated and that, when mixed in certain oils, it produced a thick liquid that could be used as lacquer and varnish. Amber, a fossilized vegetable resin, was used for the making of beads in the Oriental countries long before the empires of the Mediterranean emerged. These early people also learned that when softened resin was put into a matrix it would take on the contour of the matrix when it cooled and hardened. This was probably the birth of the molding industry.

Resins are found all over the world, and they have many uses. This, for example, for rosin—a single form of resin: It is used for making cements, varnishes, paints, sealing wax, adhesives, and some soaps; also for treating violin bows; as a dressing for machine belting; as a sizing material for paper; in the preparation of certain metals for soldering; and, in pharmacy, in some ointments, plasters, and similar preparations. Acrobats and athletes use it upon their hands and the soles of their shoes to prevent slippage.

As chemistry progressed, scientists were able to break down resins chemically and identify their components. Next, scientists learned how to reproduce resins in the laboratory, by proper blending of the components or substitute compounds. The scientists were reluctant to refer to their products as resins, so they called them resin-like products, then artificial resins, then resin substitutes, then synthetic resins. These substances were generally usable in varnishes and paints. The next step seemed obvious: if scientists could reproduce resins, they should be able to produce entirely new resin-like substances. And they were already working at this at the time when George Washington was President of the United States.

Over-simplified, the process was this. All resins contain carbon, hydrogen, and oxygen, but in a wide variety of molecular combinations. Resins contain other elements, of course, making each resin unique from others. The scientists would start out with a non-resinlike substance that contained carbon, hydrogen, and oxygen. It could be some type of plant life. It could be coal. It could be a petroleum product. With the proper levels of heat and pressure and the proper catalytic agents, the scientists could produce a molecule that became known as the "monomer" of a specific resin that existed in nature. This was the first step. Then, again with proper heat, pressure, and catalysts, the scientists could make the monomers combine into more complex compounds of themselves, and the compound became known as a "polymer" of a specific natural resin. This was the second step. The final step was to find another catalyzer—a "plasticizer" which could produce the polymer in a form that could be used by manufacturers for the making of various articles.

As always, the process seems simple when you look back on it. But even after scientists knew where they were going and that it was possible for them to succeed, it still took them a hundred years to do the job. There were so many wrong starts, so many dead ends, and the only way to go ahead was to go back and start again.

As success did come about and as new substances became available to manufacturers, the word *plastics* and the word *resins* became interchangeable, to some confusion. Generally, the plastic is the molded form of the resin—and yet not all plastics are resins, nor are all resins moldable. Some resins can be cast or converted into coatings, self-supporting films or fibers. Perhaps the confusion and misjudgment about plastics resulted from the great progress that followed, once scientists made the breakthrough from the polymers to the plastic substance itself.

People began having new words thrown at them, not

always with adequate definition. All that seemed clear was that natural substances were being replaced by some brew concocted in laboratories, and this didn't sound like much of a step forward in terms of quality. Manufacturers had a question: "Since new substances require new methods of production, where are the new methods for us to get the best return for investment in these new substances?"

Since the Stone Age, men have sought better ways to make the articles they used in their daily life. At first, they could only hammer and chisel rocks and metals. Around 4000 B.C., the Egyptians devised forging—the blacksmith's technique of using heat, a hammer, and cold water on metal. The Incas, the Aztecs, the Carthaginians, and the early Javanese had a form of die-casting—a molten substance poured into a matrix would take on the form of the matrix as it cooled and hardened. Die-casting made progress with the advent of the Industrial Revolution. Even so, the making of molds was still so primitive that it remained merely a stepping stone for industry. Molds were used to make parts of a machine that could make an article. It still was not possible to go from the raw material through a molding machine and thus to the finished article.

The molding industry really got started after the discovery in 1839 by Charles Goodyear that rubber could be vulcanized. Goodyear found that when he treated crude India rubber with sulfur compounds, under the right heat and pressure, it would become a thick liquid which could be fed through a hand-operated hydraulic press into a mold, and as it hardened it would take on the shape of the matrix. After John Hyatt developed Celluloid in 1872, he tried to use his product on this kind of press, but it didn't work. The temperature in the heating unit was too uncontrolled and varied constantly, and the temperature in the mold remained too high too long for the Celluloid to harden. Hyatt never did solve his problem.

However, Hyatt's success in turning cellulose nitrate into a widely used synthetic plastic opened the door. Within a few years, seventy-five variations on Celluloid were granted patents because in each case the inventor used a different plasticizer to make the plastic material. Viscoloid was one of these. Later, another widely accepted plastic was invented, Bakelite, named after its inventor, Dr. L. H. Baekeland, an American. Bakelite is prepared by the chemical interaction of phenolic substances, such as phenol and cresol, found in coal tar, and aldehydes, such as formaldehyde, a derivative of methyl alcohol. By 1910, the General Bakelite Company was a thriving organization. A strong substance and a non-conductor, Bakelite was being used as insulation in electric equipment, for phonograph records, and for moving parts in some machinery. Eventually, its use was expanded in the field of household items.

Now, this: Bakelite is thermosetting. This means that when the plastic is molded in any way, it retains that shape for the rest of its useful life. It cannot be returned to the viscous state by any amount of heat or any solvent. The celluloids are thermoplastic, in that a specific amount of heat and certain solvents will return them to the viscous state. All resins are either thermosetting or thermoplastic.

In 1931, the materials used by Foster Grant were thermoplastic, in sheet form. Each item had to be cut out from the sheet. Sam Foster wanted very much to make his products by casting, but no equipment was available that could do that. One afternoon, the Goodmans received a telephone call about something so exciting that they immediately put through a call to Sam at Leominster, inviting him and Joe to New York. When they walked into the Goodman office, then located at 17 West 17th Street, Manhattan, Abe Goodman said, "Sam, don't take off your hat and coat."

Sam asked, "Why not?"

Abe said, "We have to go over to Adam Bernhardt's office." The Fosters knew Adam Bernhardt. He had been with The Viscoloid Company in Leominster until the company was acquired by DuPont. Since then he had been in New York, representing German companies in the U.S. and Mexico; and he had done business occasionally with Foster Grant, but more so with the Goodmans in their other interests.

Sam asked, "It is easier for the four of us to go to see Adam than for him to come here to see us?"

Jack Goodman said, "He's just a block away, Sam. Besides, he got back from Europe yesterday and his desk is loaded."

"I'm not debating," said Sam. "I'm just asking. Let's go."

Joe Foster asked, "Adam has something for us?"

Abe shrugged, trying to be indifferent, but Jack said, "He says it could be the most important thing he's ever had for us."

Adam Bernhardt's office was at 17 East 17th Street. He had people with him when the Fosters and the Goodmans entered his office, and he immediately excused himself and hurried into the reception room. He shook hands with every-one, inquired into everyone's health, helped them remove their hats and coats, then said, "In here, please, gentlemen." He led them into a small conference room.

On the table was an assortment of plastic items—a few combs, some brushes, cutlery hands, a couple of toys, some jewelry. And Bernhardt asked, "What do you think of these?"

This was Sam's domain. He picked up each item and examined it carefully, completely, and from time to time he muttered, "Beautiful. Beautiful." Joe Foster and the Good-mans also studied the articles. Sam asked, "How were these made?"

Adam Bernhardt was grinning. "By molding machine, Sam. An *injection* molding machine." The word deserved the spotlight. John Hyatt had failed at making an injection molding machine in 1875, and everybody since who had made the effort promptly gave up in frustration. No one had tried for years. And now this.

Joe Foster asked, "Who's got the machine?"

"Eckert and Zeigler, in Germany," Bernhardt said. "The machine is so new that I couldn't find anybody in Europe who's heard about it. I understand that a few of them have been sold, but I don't know who bought them."

"Then they'll sell the machine?" Jack Goodman asked.

Adam said, "Yes."

"How much?" Abe asked.

Adam shrugged. "I didn't want to seem too interested, so I didn't press. My guess is between twenty-five hundred and three thousand."

Abe Goodman and Sam Foster exchanged a glance and

nodded at each other. Joe was examining a comb, and he asked, "What is this material?"

"That's styrene," Bernhardt said And then he saw the same question in the eyes of the four men. "It's a synthetic resin the Germans have."

Abe said, "Adam, if the top price is three thousand dollars, order ten. If it's any higher, let me know."

Adam was beaming again. He said, "I'll tell you something, Abe, Sam. Three weeks ago today, when I was at the Eckert and Zeigler plant and I saw this production and I saw the machine, I said to myself, 'This is for Foster Grant.' I said to myself, 'When I get back, I'm not going to mention this to anybody else first except Foster Grant. This is for Foster Grant!' I was that excited. It is exciting, isn't it, Sam? Abe?"

Sam said, "Let's get one of the machines over here first and try it out. Then we'll know how excited we should get."

But it was exciting. And they were excited. Their good spirits showed in their brisk gait as they crossed Fifth Avenue and went back to the Goodman office. It seemed as though a dream were about to come true, and all four of them, as they proceeded along their way, avoided the subject, as though too much talk about the wondrous machine would burst the dream bubble.

That same day they visited the New Jersey plant of the Celanese Corporation. The new machine aside, they were planning on expansion, and now they wanted to be sure of supplies. As they left Abe's car in front of the Celanese building, it was Jack who warned, "Not a word, now." And they all knew what he meant. They talked to the Celanese representative for about an hour, and then it was Jack who weak-ened.

He asked: "Do you have *styrene?*"

"The German stuff?" the man asked. Jack nodded. "No. Not yet. We've looked into it, of course, but I think we'll hold off until we get some idea of the American market."

Abe took the plunge. "Does anybody have it over here yet?"

"Why? You interested?"

Joe put in: "A friend of ours just got back from Europe. He mentioned it."

The man said, "I hear that Monsanto is looking into it, too. But I don't know if they're on stream yet."

They dropped the subject and went on to other matters for an hour, and when it became evident that the meeting was ending, it was Sam who lost his resistance. He said, "This friend of ours who just got back from Europe, he mentioned seeing an injection molding machine."

The Celanese man said, "The Eckert-Zeigler thing?"

They all winced. Sam said, "That's the one, isn't it, Joe?"

Joe said, "I think so, Dad."

The Celanese man said, "It's a pile of junk."

They all winced again. Abe said, "Really? We heard it was pretty good."

The man laughed. "You heard wrong. We couldn't even make soup with it."

"We?" asked Jack.

"Yes. Celanese. I don't know whether the think works in Germany, but I sure know it won't work over here."

Joe asked, "You've got one?"

72

"Yeah, sure," said the man. It's down in the basement. We've already dumped it. It wasn't worth the freight, let alone the three thousand bucks it cost."

"You couldn't get it working?" Abe asked.

"Not at all. We tried everything, and everything came out goo."

Sam said, "I'm sorry to hear that."

"Why?" asked the man. "You interested in the machine?"

Sam dodged the question. "I'm always sorry when nice people get stuck with a bad buy."

"Celanese can afford it," the man said. "You want a look at the thing?"

Sam returned, "Why look at something that won't work?" He wanted to get away.

Outside, they crossed the vast parking lot in silence and did not speak until they reached Abe's car. Then Jack said, "You want me to call Adam and cancel the order?"

Abe said, "That's up to Sam. Sam is the one who has to make the machine work. What do you want to do, Sam?"

Sam's expression was painful but not hopeless. He said, "Just because a machine won't work in New Jersey doesn't mean it won't work in Massachusetts. We'll get a couple of the machines and we'll see what happens."

Joe suggested, "Shouldn't Adam be tipped off, though?"

Sam said, "Why worry him? He saw the machine work in Germany. He brought back samples of the work. We all agreed it was excellent. This morning we were all excited. Let's stay a little excited. Anyway, we shouldn't want Adam to think we lost faith in him so fast." They all nodded to that. Sam said, "Joe, find out all you can about the *styrene*."

"All right, Dad."

Sam said, "Another thing. Let's not discuss this with anybody else unless we absolutely have to."

Jack said, "Right. In case the machine works, we wouldn't want anybody to beat us out."

"Not only that," said Sam. "If it doesn't work, we wouldn't want anybody to know we've been fools."

❉ ❉ ❉ ❉

Joe Foster went at his homework on styrene. And here was an intriguing facet about this young man: aside from his general science courses in high school and prep school, Joe Foster had no background in the level of chemistry to which he now turned his attention. His father's assignment had, in effect, made him like the boy scout who, having just won a merit badge in first aid, had stepped promptly up to an operating table and was expected to perform major surgery. But Joe Foster had specific assets going for him. He had always had a quick mind, a retentive memory, and an intense curiosity. He had a respect for knowledge and an admiration for the professional in any area. Though he was not mechanically inclined particularly, Joe Foster always enjoyed watching a good mechanic take apart a malfunctioning machine, find its problem, solve it, then reassemble all the parts into a working unit. Joe Foster approached his own business decisions with a similar attitude: first he examined all the parts of the issue before making a decision on the entire matter. Perhaps one aspect of law which had appealed to him in his youth was the prospect of piecing together applicable bits of evidence into a case which he could then present effectively and successfully to a jury. Now he turned to the world of petrochemistry with the determination to understand its components as well as its complete role in industry. He read avidly, everything from current professional journals to history books, and when he was not satisfied with any answers, he did not hesitate to go to the experts. The day was to come when Joseph Foster could discuss petrochemistry with the experts in their own language. The day was to come when Joe Foster would pioneer in industrial petrochemistry with confidence, courage, and the kind of curiosity that would not let him rest until he found things out for himself.

About styrene. It is the synthetic of the natural resin storax, which is found in the wood and bark of certain trees in Asia Minor and which was originally obtained by distillation of the wood and bark. The early Greeks knew it as *styrax*. Long ago, it was used medicinally, as an expectorant; it was also used in perfumes and has been used in chewing gum. Early in petrochemical research, scientists found that monomeric styrene was present in the light oils of coal-tar manufacture, but extracting the monomer from this source turned out to be too expensive to be economically practical. Moreover, the process was difficult to control. Experiments established that this monomer could be polymerized, but because of the varying quality of the monomer the end product did not seem worth further effort. Around 1870, scientists discovered that, with proper heat, proper pressure and proper catalysts, they could extract a quality monostyrene from ethylbenzene which in turn could be polymerized into quality polystyrene. However, costs were still exorbitant, and procedures were still so delicate as to be unpredictable. Not until 1911 did anyone believe that styrene would ever have any commercial value; a few patents were granted, but these were rooted more in faith than in fact. The real value of polystyrene was still to be determined. By 1931, the Germans felt they had something; the Americans were working on it. As far as Foster Grant was concerned, the high promise in polystyrene was its quick response to temperature change. Thermoplastic, it could pass from a cold solid to a molten substance and to a cold solid again in seconds, even less, and this made it perfect for injection molding. Now all that was needed was an injection molding machine that could do *its* job.

The second Eckhert and Zeigler injection molding machine arrived in the United States late in 1931. It arrived, assembled and crated, in New York by ship, addressed to the Goodmans. This was a ruse. After all, the Goodmans had machinery of their own in their New York factory and, in such a busy place, it would not be a matter of anyone's special attention that they had purchased some more. On the other hand, had the German crate been shipped directly to smaller, more neighborly Leominster, there were any number of people who might have seen it en route and might have asked: "What did you buy, Sam?" And Sam Foster did not want to tell. This way, after clearing customs, it was easy enough to paint out any revealing information, readdress the crate and ship it to Foster Grant *via Worcester*. The company men who picked up the crate by truck at Worcester had only one reaction: whatever was inside was heavy. And they wondered how often Sam Foster would have them pushing the thing around.

On the contrary, this was probably the piece of Foster Grant machinery that did the least traveling during its lifetime on Lancaster Street. Preparing for its arrival, Sam had a workroom emptied and he had a new lock put on the door to which he thereafter carried the only key. For over two years, the hallowed area beyond the locked door was to be known to all Foster Grant employees as "The Mystery Room."

When the crate arrived, Sam let the truckers struggle with it through the building to the Mystery Room, and he thanked them as they left. Then Sam sent for three or four of his best mechanics whom he had chosen because of his complete trust in their great skills and good sense. When they were with him, he asked if they would mind helping him dismantle the crate. They didn't mind. They had been with Sam long enough to know that at Foster Grant it was every man for any job. They took up crowbars and hammers and went to work. Minutes later, they had the crate dismantled; then they removed the protective packaging. And then they stared at the thing.

It was obviously a machine of some kind. It stood chest high and was about seven feet long. It was made of cast iron and steel. One end had a casing that looked like it could hold a mold. A steel tube extended from it into an elongated metal box. At mid-point, an evident hopper was connected to the box. The steel tube protruded from the box to a hinging device, to which was attached a long handle, as on a pneumatic casting machine. And that was it.

One man asked: "What is it, Sam?"

Sam said: "It is an injection molding machine."

In 1931, he could have said it was a space ship and gotten the same effect. Even experts had given up hopes for an injection molding machine. Many of them still thought injection molding was impossible. Others had not as yet thought about it at all.

So the men had many questions. Sam Foster told them everything—the work in Germany, the quality of the samples, styrene, the Celanese fiasco. Now the men were anxious to try the machine.

But Sam said: "First let's take the machine apart and get to know it well enough so that we can take it apart and put it together in our sleep. Then we will try some resins. In the meantime, this is a secret project. If I decide other people should know about it, I'll tell them. But I don't want anybody to talk about it outside of this room. Will you go along with me?"

They said they would, as Sam knew they would.

They took the machine apart and then put it together, and they did this again and again. When they started experimenting with resins, they continued to take the machine apart and then put it together, again and again, because, each time, they had to clean out the mess. Nothing worked. The art of injection molding was still so uncontrollable that even a change in the humidity could wreck an effort. There were times when Sam began to wonder if the machine had been made in such a way that it would operate only in Germany. The second machine arrived from Germany, then the third, and they wouldn't work, either.

By that time, Rudy Riesenfeld's apprehensions about his homeland materialized. Adolf Hitler had become chancellor of the country, and the persecution of the Jews had begun. The Fosters and the Goodmans talked it over. Sam still had faith in the machines, but the four men agreed that they certainly could not do business any longer with a company in a country that seemed bent on eradicating the Jewish people. Abe Goodman notified the Eckhert and Zeigler Company that the Foster Grant order for seven more injection molding machines was immediately canceled. News of this broke in the business community and then in the newspapers. Foster Grant was thus among the first, if not the first American company to take such a firm stand against the Nazis.

By that time, too, Sam Foster had made another decision. Whether the trouble with the machines was in the machines, in the air, in the resins, or in himself and his men, Sam Foster still believed that the Eckhert and Zeigler design was correct in principle. After all, the things were working in Germany. With the mystery of the Mystery Room now disclosed by the newspaper accounts of the canceled order, Sam felt there was no longer any reason to continue banging his head against the wall in secret. He decided to go to his friends in Leominster for some fresh ideas for the machines. He no longer cared about the risk of becoming a public fool. Indeed, it was more foolish to continue in the dark. Nor did he care about the risk of having some other company beat him into injection molding in the country. In the first place, with the exception of the dud in the Celanese basement, he had the only machines in the United States that could pass for injection molding machines, which gave him a good lead.

And in the second place, if anybody beat him out, well, more power to him.

Among others, Sam and Joe went to see Morris Falk, head of the Independent Lock Company. Independent was die-casting its products. Its engineering expert was Phil Graham. Falk sent for him, and the Fosters again told their story.

Then Graham said, "The machines are pneumatic, are they? We're on hydraulic machines here. It seems to me that the basic principles in die-casting and injection molding are quite a bit alike. What do you think of changing your machines to hydraulic power?"

"You think it can be done?" Sam asked.

"It's certainly worth a try," Graham said.

Sam turned to Morris Falk. "Morris, can I borrow this man for a while?" Falk said yes.

Another borrowed man was Harold Farnsworth, who had been with the Leominster Tool Company. Farnsworth thought there might be something wrong with the feeder system, and so he invented a separation nozzle which controlled the fluidity of the liquid resin as it entered the mold. Another troublesome spot was the heating unit. Thermoplastics could begin to harden at the slightest drop in temperature, and this was sometimes happening within the heating unit itself, causing the machine to jam. Foster Grant men and Farnsworth worked together to devise an insulation for the heating unit to keep the temperature constant throughout.

It went like that—a little progress here, a little progress there, sometimes the idea of one man, sometimes the idea of several, often the result of Sam Foster's incessant "Can we try this?" and "Can we move this over here?" and "Will it help if you turn this piece upside down?" Late in 1933, two years after receiving its first Eckhert-Zeigler, Foster Grant had operable injection molding machines, the only ones in the country, and they bore as much resemblance to the German import as a Rolls-Royce bears to a Model T. But nobody was satisfied with the quality of the product, so months more of work went into the machines.

Thus it was in 1934 that Foster Grant began to market the first injection-molded articles made in the United States —combs and sunglasses. In the old days, a good worker could turn out five dozen combs a day by hand. Now the machines were making that many in a minute. In the old days, a half-dozen good workers took all day to turn out by hand the parts for two gross of sunglasses. Now that machine could do it in an hour.

Even so, there was not a moment when the people at Foster Grant could sit back and say, "There. That's it. The job is done." Over the next four or five years, the Foster Grant technicians made seventy-eight injection molding machines from the floor up, and no two were alike. A new department had to be established. Eighty-five expert mechanics had to be rounded up from across the country. No matter how experienced these men were, when they went to work on injection molding machines, they were novices, because these machines were a new breed in industry. And yet this was a good thing. Men with imagination and with creativity could get very excited about these new machines and would then come up with their own ideas for improvements. Men whose skills were enough to bring them top salaries started hanging around the shops at night on their own, turning into inventors. Sometimes parts of a new machine would be jobbed out to a Leominster foundry, and there were times when the jobber would call Foster Grant and ask, "Are you guys sure you know what you're doing? I don't think this thing you've sent over here can really be made." And the Foster Grant man would say, "Oh, hell, I'll come over there and draw pictures for you." Usually an innovation was so unique that the Foster Grant technician who thought of it would just go into the tool-and-die section and sit down and go to work. The stimulating atmosphere at Foster Grant of growth and progress was conducive to that kind of initiative.

The day did come, however, when the Fosters and the Goodmans had to make a decision about these new machines. Undoubtedly, Foster Grant had given the country—the world, perhaps—a new industry. Should Foster Grant go into manufacturing injection molding machines, or should the company remain in the business of producing articles by injection molding? The Fosters and the Goodmans agreed to remain in the field of articles.

Some of the men who had worked at Foster Grant during the three years of experimentation went into the manufacture of the machines and equipment, and they were very successful. Today, the injection molding industry is just as common across the United States as assembly-line production. This might not have been so—at least, it would certainly have been different—had not Sam and Joe Foster and Abe and Jack Goodman been the sort of men who refused to take no for an answer from the experts or from a machine or from themselves.

82

5

The National Pyralart Company of Mexico remained a Foster Grant affiliate for over twenty years. In 1939, injection molding was introduced at the Monterrey plant. The company continued to grow throughout the years of World War II. After the war, Foster Grant began to expand into the new area of plastic, and each year Joe Foster found that he had less time to devote to the Mexican operation. In 1957, he sold the Monterrey company to Mexican interests.

During this span of years, Foster Grant became affiliated with other companies in other countries. One such affiliation was with M. Winthrop and Sons, of Toronto, Canada. The Goodmans had previously had a working arrangement with the Winthrops, and so, after the Foster-Goodman partnership in 1929, it followed that Foster Grant should become involved a couple of years later. At first, the relationship was a matter of distributing each other's non-competitive items in each other's country. With the advent of injection molding at Leominster, Foster Grant manufactured articles for the Winthrop line. The association was a good one, personal and friendly. The Winthrops—father and two sons—were, like the Fosters and the Goodmans, totally devoted to their company, their social and business lives intertwining. The three-way limited partnership enjoyed a healthy growth for twenty years, when, in the Fifties, and for the same reasons he withdrew from Mexico, Joe Foster was too occupied with other expansion activities and therefore yielded his holdings in the partnership to the Winthrops.

Another such affiliation began in 1936, this time with Laughton and Sons, Ltd., of Birmingham, England. This was an old company, having been established in 1860 as Jarrett and Rainsford, pin manufacturers and merchants. Jarrett withdrew after a few years, and the company remained in the Rainsford family. George A. Laughton was fifteen when he went to work for the company in 1898. By 1928, he was at the executive level and had acquired a controlling interest from the Rainsford family. Meanwhile, the company had expanded into combs and hair ornaments.

In 1936, Laughton, by then head of the company, had visited its facilities in Australia and was returning to England via the United States. He had been interested in adding a hair-curler to his line. In New York, he mentioned this to a friend, and the friend happened to know Abe Goodman, who had a line of curlers in his own company. Goodman and Laughton were brought together.

They had only two hours together, but in that short time Abe Goodman was able to convince George Laughton that injection molding, now in production at Foster Grant, was going to revolutionize industry. Next morning, Laughton left for England ready to introduce injection molding into his country. Two weeks later, Abe Goodman went to Birmingham. A new company—TWINCO—was formed, half of it owned by Laughton, half by the Goodmans and the Fosters. Because nobody in England knew anything about injection molding machines, Laughton chose his grandson, Malcolm, then just nineteen, to go to Leominster to find out about them. During the year young Malcolm spent in Massachusetts, he became caught up in the Foster Grant spirit of inventiveness, and several patents are to his credit.

By the end of 1937, when Malcolm was ready to go home, four Foster Grant injection molding machines had already been shipped over and were installed in a new factory appropriately called the Leominster Works. The Foster Grant machines weathered the Atlantic crossing far better than had the Eckhert-Zeiglers. Once the staff at the Leominster Works got the feel of them, they were giving top performance.

As the pioneer of injection molding in England, TWINCO got off to a fast start. At first, the resin—vinyl acetate—was also shipped over by Foster Grant, but British production was soon established by other companies there.

There was every likelihood that TWINCO would become a leader in British industry; but then, in September, 1939, England went to war against Germany, and during a Nazi air strike on Birmingham the following year the Leominster Works was badly hit and put out of operation. Not until 1947 were the molding machines uncovered from the ruins and put back to work. By then, money was tight on both sides of the Atlantic. The American partners had difficulty transferring funds for the reconstruction of the Leominster Works. At the same time, the British partners realized that the international flavor of TWINCO was creating some obstacles in their efforts for British government aid in reconstruction. For these reasons, TWINCO was dissolved and the Laughton company proceeded with injection molding as an integral part of its own firm.

In 1968, tight money again was the factor which curtailed Foster Grant expansion on the international horizon. The company interests which influenced Joe Foster's withdrawal from Mexico and Canada ten years previous had been the Foster Grant growth in the plastics industry. By 1966, Foster Grant was among the front runners in the U.S. production of resins. That year, Foster Grant and Farbwerke Hoechst A.G., of Frankfurt, West Germany, one of the world's largest producers of plastics, formed a joint venture for the expanded production of polystyrene in Europe. Called Polymeerfabrieken Breda, the new company took over a polymerization plant which had already been constructed by Foster Grant in Breda, The Netherlands. This plant, while small, was producing a line of plastics which in but a few short years had achieved acceptance among the largest

European plastic product manufacturers. Anxious to acquire this know-how and technology, Farbwerke Hoechst acquired a 50% interest in this facility and the new company began the construction of the largest polystyrene plant in Europe. Within a year, however, the drain on the U.S. gold supply had grown so serious that President Lyndon B. Johnson asked American industrialists to reconsider any plans they had for heavy investments abroad. It was in compliance with this presidential request that Joe Foster asked his German partners to release him from their oint venture. But this change of plans did not, by any means, indicate any change of heart in the Foster Grant impetus for growth, not by any means at all.

*　*　*　*

There was a sidelight to the Mexican venture that still sends shivers through those who were even indirectly involved in it. Harry Bergman died in 1934, and it became necessary for Sam Foster to go back to Monterrey to find someone to supervise the operation. While there, Sam heard the rampant rumors about the fortunes in silver just waiting to be picked up off the ground in the mountains. The silver was actually scraps, called tailings, which had been discarded as not worth smelting in the days when the mines were being worked. Some of the mines had been exhausted; others had been abandoned by owners who turned out to be on the wrong side when the Mexican revolution ended. Rumor had it that the natives were making a good living by going into the mountains to the mines, filling a few sacks with tailings, and selling them to silversmiths in town.

Sam Foster never gave much thought to getting rich quick, but he could rarely resist whatever struck him as a good investment. The U.S. had just lowered the gold content of its coins, sending the price of gold up from $20.66 to $35 an ounce. In turn, this sent the price of silver up. Sam felt that if the tailings could really be gathered by the bucketful, it would be a mistake not to go after it. Some of the silver could be used to decorate Foster Grant articles at great savings, and the rest could be sold. This was too good to pass up.

Sam had heard that the best area for tailings was Aguascalientes, in the west central part of the country, north of Mexico City. He went there. After talks with local experts, he got together an expedition. The mine most recommended to him had been owned by a Mexican family that had moved to New York. It was eighty miles into the mountains—as the crow flies—but the curving mountain roads made the distance almost three times that. Sam was no longer a young man, and he had never been particularly physical, but he insisted on making the journey that took over a week. By day, he spent most of his time on horseback. Meals were canned meat and beans and rice, cooked over a wayside fire. At night, he slept between blankets under the open skies. He thrived on it, never feeling better in his life. He felt even better when he saw the mounds of tailings around the mine. And he couldn't have felt better when experts at Aguascalientes and Denver assured him that the tailings contained a high percentage of good quality silver.

Sam Foster was on fire when he got back to Leominster. He persuaded some friends to invest in a syndicate with him. Sam hurried back to Mexico with the money. Meanwhile, Joe Foster went to New York and acquired rights to the mine from the owners for fifteen thousand dollars plus a percentage. And that was the end of the good part.

In Aguascalientes, Sam Foster discovered that equipping a proper expedition to work the mine was going to cost three times more than had originally been estimated. The price of extracting the silver from the tailings also turned out to be much higher than anybody expected. But having gone this far, Sam felt he might as well go on, depending on a high return to make up the differences. The working crew had been at the mine only a few days when news came down the mountains that the camp had been attacked by bandits, the Chinese cook had been killed, and the chief engineer had been kidnapped and was being held for ten thousand dollars ransom.

Not knowing where Sam was, the Aguascalientes authorities telephoned the news to Monterrey. Nobody at Monterrey knew where Sam was, so the news was telephoned to Leominster. Joe Foster didn't know where his father was. For hours, there was panic in Aguascalientes, in Monterrey, and in Leominster, for fear Sam had decided at the last moment to go along on the expedition.

Then Sam Foster came strolling into his Monterrey office, not all smiles but yet not discouraged, and completely unaware of what had happened in the mountains. First he called Joe to let him know he was safe. Then he turned around and headed back to Aguascalientes to see what could be done about the engineer. What was done was familiar Mexican procedure. The area was sparsely settled, and everybody knew everybody. A lot of people knew who the bandits were. Police rounded up relatives of the bandits, put them in jail, then sent word into the mountains that the relatives would stay in jail until the bandits released the engineer. A few days later, the haggard engineer came walking into town alone.

It was all over. Too much had been lost to go on. The only comfort in it was that Sam Foster had not gone on that second expedition. Back in Leominster, Sam personally absorbed most of the lost investment. People tried to put the experience out of their minds. After such a misadventure, most men would have been willing to find a quiet corner for the rest of their lives. But not Sam Foster.

❊   ❊   ❊   ❊

He needed some elbow room. This was in 1936, and Sam Foster was complaining that he could not squeeze one more square inch of space out of the Lancaster Street factory. The company would have to move into larger quarters. Joe acknowledged that his father was right, but when he found out which property in Leominster Sam had in mind, he suddenly was not so sure.

The property was out on North Main Street, at the edge of town, and for years it had been the site of the Richardson Piano Case Company. At one time, Leominster had three or four companies that made the wooden portion of pianos, shipping the sections elsewhere for assembly and installation of the other parts of the instrument. With time, the radio replaced the piano as the American family's main source of entertainment in the home. One by one, the Leominster piano case factories shut down. In an effort to keep up with the times, the Richardson company turned to making radio cabinets. But the company was late getting into the field; it got caught in a price war, and one day the Richardson family filed for bankruptcy Leominster was still feeling the grip of the Depression in 1936, and there were a number of empty factory buildings in town, any one of which suited Joe as the new home for Foster Grant. Sam Foster wanted the Richardson property.

The main building was a huge, four-story structure with floor space of a hundred sixty-five thousand square feet. Adjacent to it was a two-story frame building which the Richardsons had first used as a home and then as an office. The property covered sixty-five acres, with four smaller buildings on it. The whole layout was available for thirty-six thousand dollars.

Joe said, "Dad, you're going overboard. The main building alone is four times bigger than our three buildings on Lancaster Street put together."

"I know," said Sam. "It's a wonderful bargain."

"But what are we going to do with all that room?" Joe asked.

Sam said, "Calm down, Joe. The day will come when you'll need more room."

That settled it. Foster Grant moved into its new home on August 21, 22, and 23. When all the equipment was placed to Sam's satisfaction, it covered most of the first floor and part of the second floor. The third floor became a warehouse. Joe asked, "Dad, what do you want to do with the top floor?"

"I'll think of something," said Sam. "For now, we can use it for company dances."

"We can use it for company baseball," said Joe.

They used the small house as the office, and it was too big, too. By then, Foster Grant had about four hundred employees in the factory, but only five or six in the office. Sam still disliked paperwork, and he was glad that Joe seemed to have a good mind for it, handling it quickly and effectively. Actually, Joe was not overly fond of paperwork himself. He much preferred being on the road, selling. But during the years Sam spent so much time in the Mystery Room, Joe found himself taking the telephone calls and answering the mail. And while Sam was in Mexico, Joe ran the company simply because there was no one else to run it. By 1936, Sam Foster had virtually phased himself out of the administration side of Foster Grant affairs. He was still the head of the company and made the ultimate decisions, but the responsibility for making Foster Grant function smoothly as a business entity moved more and more to Joe's desk. Sam was content to have this huge building to roam through, as he had once roamed through the tiny hovel on Manning Avenue, and the day was not far off when he would seek an even wider world.

6

In the Golden Anniversary Year of 1969, Joseph C. Foster, chairman of the board of Foster Grant, would still say that he preferred to be on the road, selling. He would say, "There is more to selling than just making your pitch, getting the order, then rushing off to the next stop. A good salesman has a sincere respect for buyers. He regards them as friends. He has faith in his products, and so he knows that a sale will do as much good for the customer as it will for his own company. A good business relationship has to have its personal side. Both the salesman and the buyer must want each other to come out ahead. That's what makes selling meaningful. I've always enjoyed the road. I like knowing that I've got friends in every town in the country."

Perhaps a man has to be born with this attitude. Certainly, traveling salesmen are a special breed. To be willing to spend weeks on the road, away from one's family, spending each night in a different hotel, living out of suitcases, eating dinners some hotel chef cooked that morning, waiting hours in reception rooms to see a buyer and more hours at airports to catch a plane to the next buyer—all this requires a specific dedication. Perhaps good salesmen are like zealous missionaries for whom a first sale to a new buyer is a kind of conversion.

Milton W. Bernstein, Foster Grant vice president in charge of sunglass sales, has put it this way: "A good salesman is distinctly individual. He has to be different. If he's like everybody else, he's a bum. He must be excited about his line, proud of it, and he must be able to transmit the excitement and pride to the buyer. Selling is mostly a matter of marketing. A salesman not only does a selling job for his company, but he has to be ready to go that extra mile by doing a selling job for the customer as well."

Milt Bernstein had an early experience with two-way selling. It was in 1939. He had been with Foster Grant about a year. At the time, sunglasses were displayed in stores either on a card or just loose in a box on the counter. Also at the time, sunglasses were still a novelty. People didn't wake up in the morning and say, "I've got to buy some sunglasses today." But when they came upon sunglasses in a shop, they were apt to browse, consider, even buy. Milt Bernstein felt that shoppers would pay more attention to sunglasses if sunglasses were getting more attention in the shop. And the best kind of attention, he knew, would be a window display. To the best of his knowledge, there had never been an entire window display just of sunglasses.

In New York, Bernstein called on a buyer he knew at the Woolworth Company and brought up the idea of a window display. The buyer said, "Well, Milt, as you know, we leave the matter of window displays to the individual store managers. They know best what they want to promote in their areas, and we don't interfere."

"Yes, I do know that," said Milt, "but I wanted your okay first before I approach any of them."

"That's no problem. I'll have my secretary prepare a letter."

"Thanks."

The buyer asked, "Where are you planning to try your luck?"

"Atlantic City," said Milt. "In July. Lots of people will be there then, for the sun, and they ought to be wearing sunglasses."

"We've got a store just off the Boardwalk," the buyer said.

Milt said, "That's the one I want."

A few days later, Milt Bernstein was in the Atlantic City store. He introduced himself to the manager, presented the letter from the buyer, and then said, "Now, sir, I understand that what goes into your windows is entirely up to you. I talked to your people in New York first just in case you had any doubts about how they might feel. I know I'm asking for something unusual."

"You sure are," said the manager. "I've never given a whole window to just one item before."

"It would be more than one item," Milt assured. "We've got a dozen different types of sunglasses. They'd make an effective display. And at this time of the year, you'll do a good business."

"Maybe," the manager conceded. "But how would we display them—on your cards and in the boxes?"

"Why not leave that to me?" Milt suggested. "You tell me when I can have a window. I'll be here that day. I'll bring all my own equipment. I'll install the display myself. If I need any of your people, I'll pay for their time. And whenever you want to change the window, I'll come back and remove my stuff."

"That's a fair deal," the man admitted.

They chose the day.

By 1939, Foster Grant had solved most of its problems with the lenses for sunglasses. The tinted window glass had been discarded long before. For a while, the company ordered tinted lenses from Japan. But the Japanese line was limited, the quality was inconsistent, and delivery was uncertain. Operating in a small town in West Virginia was the L. J. Houze Company, a family of Belgian glassblowers that had moved to America after World War I and gone into business. The Houze family specialized in glassware but, expanding, they began making colored lenses for Wilson

Products, of Pennsylvania, one of the first American companies to make sunglasses. Joe Foster made contact with the Houze family, inspected a variety of their lenses, and then gave them an order. The convenience of working with an American company was soon threatened by production problems. The Houzes were artists who would not be rushed, so there were delivery delays. They had their own way of doing things, so the delivered lenses were not always what had been ordered. And they were expensive. Foster Grant turned back to Japan for its supply. Around 1937, the Houze Company hired as general manager a man named Cliff Frye, and Frye wanted to get the Foster Grant account back. He went to Leominster and had a long talk with Joe Foster. Joe agreed to go to West Virginia to meet the Houzes and perhaps work out some equitable arrangement. The trip was a great success. The experience of a face-to-face meeting, of dining in the Houze home and spending an evening at cards with them, was enough to establish the kind of rapport Joe Foster felt necessary in business relationships. And there was an even better turn of events. The Houzes had devised a new technique for making lenses. They shaped the colored glass into balls ranging from eighteen inches to thirty-four inches in diameter. To make lenses of any desired size or shape, Foster Grant had only to "shave" the glass from the surface of the balls. It was a great idea.

Milton Bernstein had those balls in mind when he got his idea for a window display. Shortly before the day he was to install the display in the Atlantic City store, he telephoned the Houzes and asked them to ship to the store two or three dozen of the balls of all colors and sizes. The crates were awaiting Milt when he got to the store. Immediately he had a problem: the larger balls could not pass through the narrow door that opened onto the display area.

He went to the store manager and said, "I can't get some of the big balls through that little door."

The man said, "I hope you don't expect me to tear the wall down for you."

"No, that won't be necessary," said Bernstein. "But will it be all right if I get some glaziers to remove the plate glass from the outside? That way, I can get all the balls inside, and the glaziers can replace the glass."

"Will you pay for any plate glass that gets broken?" the manager asked.

Milt said, "Of course."

"All right, then."

It took an hour to find some glaziers who would do the emergency job, another hour for them to show up, another hour to remove the plate glass. Milt had all the balls in the window in minutes, and then the glaziers took another hour to replace the glass. Milt's inventiveness cost Foster Grant an unexpected seventy-five dollars for the glaziers. Because of the lost time, Milt had to hire—at overtime rates—two of the store's decorators in order to finish the display before the store had to be locked up. That cost another fifty.

But it was worth it. Some of the sunglasses were placed on the floor in careful disarray. Others hung from the ceiling on colored strings. Others were affixed to the balls with Scotch tape. When the lights were properly adjusted, the display became a glittering rainbow. Crowds gathered at the window even before the job was done. All evening, Milt stood outside the store, glowing inwardly as crowds continued to gather at the window and admire the display. Next morning, more people were there. Milt Bernstein continued to glow as he watched one stroller after another pause at the window, study the display, nod decisively, and then go inside and buy a pair of sunglasses. Milt was able to go back on the road with a very light heart.

Two weeks later, as agreed, Milt was back at the store to take out the display. When he entered the store, the manager greeted him with a big wave and a big grin. Milt asked, "How did it go?"

"Just great," said the man. "We've had a regular run on your sunglasses."

"I'm glad to hear that," Milt said.

"In fact I'll need more. Our busiest season is still ahead of us."

"I'm glad to hear that, too," Milt said. "Now, give me a minute to get my stuff out of your window and then I'll take your order."

Milt went into the window, gathered all the sunglasses and put them into boxes. And then he wondered what in hell to do with all those glass balls. They weren't worth shipping back to West Virginia. They had been handled and rolled around so much during the installation of the display that undoubtedly they were damaged beyond use for lenses, so there was no sense shipping them to Leominster. And Milt swore that he wasn't about to pay glaziers another seventy-five bucks to remove the plate glass for the five minutes he would need to take out the balls.

He went back to the store manager. "Have you got any empty boxes?"

"There should be some in the back."

"And do you happen to have a sledge hammer?"

"I think there's a sledge hammer in the back, too."

Milt got the boxes and the sledge hammer and went back into the window. Standing there in full view, he placed the balls one by one into the empty boxes and then, using the sledge hammer, proceeded to smash the balls to smithereens. He drew the biggest crowd in the store's history.

It was another window display, at the other end of the country, that led Foster Grant into an entirely new era of merchandising sunglasses. This was in 1945. That year, Joe Foster went to California to confer with Joe Hale, who had a sales agency in Los Angeles and handled Foster Grant products for the West Coast. Joe Foster and Joe Hale had met several years previous in New England. Hale was then with a Vermont pencil company; the two men met at a trade exhibition for the region, and they struck up a friendship.

Later, Joe Hale went to Chicago with the Dixon Pencil Company. A company engineer designed a new mechanical pencil with a concave tip which would allow a person to use it for longer periods without getting writer's cramp. The engineer suggested that the tip should be made by injection molding. Joe Hale took the pencil to Joe Foster at Leominster and asked if Foster Grant could mold the tip. It was a tricky job, demanding the utmost precision. Not only must each tip fit the body of the pencil, but the tiny opening in the crown had to be perfectly aligned to the inner mechanical parts. Between designers at Dixon and Foster Grant, a mold was made. This was the first custom molding assignment Foster Grant accepted, and the company turned out millions of the tips, each one perfect.

Next, Joe Hale bought the Los Angeles sales agency and moved out there. Among the lines he handled were the sunglasses put out by Wilson Products, an expensive line, with prices ranging between fifteen and twenty-five dollars. Foster Grant sunglasses were selling for as little as thirty-nine cents in variety stores and from one to three dollars in drugstores and specialty shops. The company had already achieved national distribution. One day Joe Hale saw some Foster Grant sunglasses—called Grantly's—in a California store. He telephoned Joe Foster and asked, "How about letting me handle your line out here?"

Joe Foster asked, "Aren't you already handling the Wilson line?"

"I am," said Hale, "but so what?"

"A lot of companies don't like their sales rep to carry competitive lines," Joe Foster pointed out.

"Does it make any difference to you?" Hale asked.

"Not in the least."

"All right. I'll find out how Wilson feels about it."

Wilson didn't like it. Joe Hale therefore withdrew from the Wilson account and turned to Foster Grant. The less expensive sunglasses opened new outlets for Hale, thereby also finding new customers for other products he handled.

On Joe Foster's 1945 trip to California, Hale said to him, "The other day I saw something in a specialty shop that I think would interest you." When Joe asked what it was, Hale said, "I think it'll be more effective if I just show it to you."

It turned out to be a window display of sunglasses. The display man had stretched about fifteen feet of chicken wire across the window and perched the sunglasses on it by inserting the temples through the holes in the wire. Joe Foster said, "That's very clever. I wonder what made him think of it? Let's find out."

In the shop, the display director explained, "The boss wanted some sunglasses in the window, and I decided the only way to make an effective display was to put in dozens of them. At first I thought of just punching holes in cardboard and sticking the temples through, but that didn't have any flair. So I hunted around the basement and found the chicken wire."

"You're a resourceful man," Joe said. "If you think of some way my company can display sunglasses that well on a counter, let me know."

Joe never heard from the man, but he couldn't get the idea out of his mind. Good counter displays for sunglasses were an old problem. The cards were not satisfactory. If a shopper decided against a pair he had removed from the card to try on, it was almost impossible to replace the glasses on the card. And the boxes and tubs were also unsatisfactory. People had to fish through the pile for a pair they might buy, usually smudging lenses and sometimes damaging frames in the process. What was needed was some sort of holder on which the sunglasses could be attractively displayed, easily removed, and easily replaced, and the holder should fit on a counter.

On the trip East, Joe spent most of his time doodling. Chicken wire was out of the question, of course, and yet chicken wire held the right concept. Joe doodled some more. By the time he reached Leominster, he had a design he felt might work. It looked like an octagonal hatbox made from an Erector Set, with the vertical and horizontal rods positioned at distances that produced rectangles of space just big enough to hold a pair of sunglasses with the temples extended inward, and the thing revolved on a center pole. Joe had the feeling that something was missing; he realized that people usually try on two or three pairs of glasses before making a choice, so he added a mirror.

This crude sketch developed into the now famous Foster Grant revolving carrousel, and it added Joe's name to the list of Foster Grant patent-holding inventors. Foster Grant artists and designers added the flair that made the carrousel an instant hit. Molds were made to produce the framework rods from resins by injection molding, and the rods were designed to snap together firmly enough to withstand a bump or even being knocked over in a crowded store. A decision had to be made whether to ship a carrousel to a store in pieces or already assembled and with the sunglasses in place. For customer convenience, the carrousels were shipped assembled, ready to go on display as soon as they were removed from the box. What about costs? Though the carrousels meant a new department, hiring more people, additional production and packaging, Joe Foster decided that the company would benefit so greatly from this important attention-getter that the carrousels should be supplied to the stores free of charge. The first counter models held either four or six dozen sunglasses; the first floor models could hold twelve dozen. Later counter models held sixteen dozen; and floor models had room for as many as a hundred eighteen dozen, with storage space for more.

All this from chicken wire.

Joe Foster admits, "The simplest ideas can be the best."

❁ ❁ ❁ ❁

The Foster Grant sales division began to take permanent shape in mid-1933, around the time when doubts about the injection molding machines were being overcome and quality control remained the only problem. By then, the two or three salesmen Joe Foster had hired had gone on to other jobs. And Harry C. Richards, Sr., had come into the picture.

Harry Richards had been with Butler Brothers, the wholesalers, who then also operated the Ben Franklin stores. Richards was in sales, but on the inside, at the Jersey City, New Jersey, office, and his main job was to keep up the inventory on sales and purchases by men on the outside. Richards wanted to get on the outside.

The first contact between Joe Foster and Harry Richards grew out of sunglass sales Joe had made to Butler Brothers. In the course of his job, Richards had occasion to telephone Joe. When business took Joe Foster into the Butler Brothers office, he would stop and chat with Richards. One day in 1932, Richards asked, "Hey, Joe, do you have a place for me in your organization?"

Joe thought he was kidding. "You want to come to Foster Grant?"

"Maybe."

Joe laughed. "I'm sure we can't afford you."

"Maybe you can. I want to go into selling, Joe."

"Why don't you sell here?"

"I've talked to a few people," Richards said, "but the sales force is full these days. So I'm in the market for another job."

Joe saw Richards was serious. "Well, Harry," he said, "with all the contacts you have in this business, I'm sure you'd be an asset to any company. But Foster Grant has a lot of money tied up in some new machines we're trying to develop, and I'm sure we can't meet your price, Harry."

"What price can you meet, Joe?" Harry asked. Joe told him. Harry asked, "Plus commission?"

"Yes."

"When do I go to work?"

Everybody at Foster Grant in the Golden Anniversary Year enthusiastically accredited Harry Richards as the man who put Foster Grant on the map. He had a lot of good contacts in the various areas of retailing, yes, but equally important, the man was a born salesman. His friendliness was contagious; he effused confidence; his zeal would have been overpowering had it not been so pleasant to observe. And he had always been this way. At Butler Brothers, he often worked with men in other companies who were on their way up the ladder, and he treated them with the same respect and directness that he did their bosses. When these men got to the top, their doors were always open to Harry Richards. Now Harry headed for those doors.

He took office space in the Goodmans' building, at 17 W. 17th Street. Joe Foster accompanied Richards on his initial calls on his contacts, and there was good reason for this. Joe knew the line better, he knew production, and he was in a more knowledgeable position for on-the-spot negotiations. In time, Harry Richards became equally qualified in these areas, but he was so anxious to start selling that he asked Joe to travel with him across the country to make the presentation after Harry made the introduction to his old friends.

It was during this early period that Foster Grant acquired its first sales representative, in New York. He was Charles Jacobsen, and his special value to Foster Grant was his excellent reputation among the giant brokers, wholesalers, and distributors whose massive sales forces sold directly to the thousands of independent stores of all kinds in the country that were potential outlets for Foster Grant. One of these giants was McKesson and Robbins, specialists in drug supplies and related articles to over thirty thousand pharmacies.

Earlier, McKesson and Robbins had notified Jacobsen that they were in the market for a line of sunglasses they could merchandise as their own brand. Working for Jacobsen was a salesman who had once been on the road for an optical company that made celluloid frames. The man simply went back to his old boss and made the deal; the optical company bought some tinted lenses and then settled back to enjoy the new revenue. The glasses were all right, but after Charles Jacobsen saw the Foster Grants he knew the two lines were not in the same class. He instructed his assistant to take some Foster Grants to William Blanc, the buyer at McKesson and Robbins, with the suggestion that Blanc consider changing manufacturers. The assistant returned with the news that Blanc had decided to keep things as they were. Jacobsen couldn't understand this. He was the sort of salesman who had a protective interest for both parties in a transaction, and he couldn't understand why Bill Blanc would prefer an obviously inferior item. A week later, Jacobsen himself took Foster Grant samples to Blanc. In the first moments of the conversation, Jacobsen realized that, though Blanc had heard about the new line, this was the first time he was seeing samples. Blanc's decision was predictable: he switched to Foster Grant. Jacobsen confronted his assistant with his oversight and was then satisfied that the man had no reason for holding back the Foster Grant samples except loyalty to his former employer. In the Golden Anniversary Year, Foster Grant was still putting out a special line called No-Glair—for McKesson and Robbins.

Foster Grant relations with another buyer did not get off to the same happy start. This was a Woolworth man; his name was Charles Lyman, and he was an expert in jewelry. In 1936, Lyman was made head buyer of jewelry in the New York office, and he also found himself responsible for sunglasses. Though sunglasses were becoming Foster Grant's major item, the company was still making jewelry, and this meant working directly with Charles Lyman with both lines. There was no problem with the sunglasses. Usually, Lyman ordered by mail, from the catalog. But jewelry was another matter. Because jewelry was an impulse item—women bought it because it caught their eye—it was necessary to bring out new pieces continually, and this, in turn, required frequent calls upon the buyers.

Charles Lyman's position at Woolworth made him one of the most important buyers in the country. It was therefore good form and proper courtesy for the two top salesmen at

Foster Grant to respectfully call on him together. The first time Joe Foster and Harry Richards entered Lyman's office with their new line of jewelry, Lyman was signing his mail and did not look up as they crossed the room to him. For several moments, Joe and Harry hovered a few feet from Lyman's desk, waiting. Joe was expecting Lyman to suggest that they take seats, but he didn't.

Finally, Lyman leaned back, looked at them with a blank expression, and asked, "Well, boys, what have you got for me today?"

They put their sample cases on the floor and opened them. Joe brought up a tray of jewelry and, with a smile and a hope, handed it to Charles Lyman. Lyman took the tray, studied it briefly, and then he actually threw the tray at Joe's head. Joe caught it and shot a puzzled glance at Lyman, looking for the joke. Lyman was looking at Harry Richards expectantly. Harry passed a tray to Lyman, and almost immediately it came sailing back at him. Harry missed it and stooped to retrieve it, and as he straightened, he had to duck to miss the next tray on its return flight from Lyman's hands. This went on for fifteen minutes, with tray after tray being pitched back either to Joe or Harry.

Then Joe said, "That's all we've got this time, Mr. Lyman."

Lyman said, "Sorry—nothing I can use. See you on the next trip, boys."

Out in the hall, Harry said, "What the hell was that all about?"

"I don't know," said Joe. "He's dangerous."

"Do you think he's always like that?"

"Maybe he's had a bad day."

"Well," said Harry, "it's a strange way for a man to behave."

For over a year, Charles Lyman behaved in the same strange way each time Joe and Harry called on him every couple of months. He never asked them to sit down. His opening question was always the same, "Well, boys, what have you got for me today?" And then whatever they had was sent flying back at them. They did not make a single sale. If it weren't for the fact that Charles Lyman continued to buy Foster Grant sunglasses, Joe and Harry might have felt that they had run into one of those inexplicable personality conflicts that sometimes develop between men on sight, and they would try to live with it. But they couldn't figure the man out. All they knew was that they were becoming very adept at fielding line drives.

Then one day Joe and Harry were with a friend, another salesman, when Lyman's name came up, and Joe told about the unusual experience he and Harry were having with the man. The friend laughed. "Hasn't anybody told you?"

"Told us what?" Joe asked.

"Charlie Lyman is okay. For my money, he's just about the best jewelry buyer in the business. But all he wants to handle is jewelry. Ever since Woolworth put him on sunglasses, too, he hasn't missed a chance to let people know that he doesn't like it at all. It's the talk of the office. Well, you guys are in sunglasses. That's probably why he's been a little rough on you. Give him some time. He'll get used to it."

On the next two calls, Charles Lyman was as he had

been before. And then suddenly he changed. Next time Joe and Harry entered Lyman's office, he rose to greet them. He shook hands with them and called them by their first names. He invited them to sit down. They chatted a few minutes about nothing special. Then Lyman asked, "Well, boys, what have you got for me today?" Joe and Harry braced themselves. Joe handed over the first tray. Lyman studied it, then said, "I like these. Yes, this is good work. I think we can use some. What else have you got?"

That was it. Spring training was over. Without discussion or explanation, the past peculiar year was dismissed completely, as though it had never happened. A few years later, however, Joe and Harry learned from Charles Lyman that a buyer, even a buyer who had become a friend, was nevertheless an individual who must be allowed his moods and whims, and salesmen just had to live with it. Milton Bernstein was in on this.

Joe's mother and Milt's mother were sisters. Milt's father had a bakery in Schenectady, New York, and so during their youth the two cousins usually saw each other only at family gatherings and holidays. After high school, Milton entered the Albany, New York, College of Pharmacy, receiving his degree and license in 1931. Since then, Milt kept up his license, but he never got to practice his profession. Soon after leaving college, he acquired a summer camp which provided him with a comfortable living for several years. Then he began to feel a need for change. In 1938, he and Joe were together at a family gathering. They talked about their businesses. Listening to Joe, Milt found himself intrigued by Joe's accounts of selling, and he indicated that he would like to try something like that himself. Joe suggested that Milt go to New York and talk to Harry Richards. Milt did, and he was hired. It was Harry Richards idea that Milt would benefit from a good foundation in Foster Grant production methods, and so Milt spent most of his first year with the company at the factory in Leominster. He took his first road trips with Harry Richards. His first sales were to branch stores of Foster Grant outlets in the Midwest.

Late in 1940, Joe Foster suggested that Milt accompany him and Harry on another call on Charles Lyman. Foster Grant was about to bring out a new line of floral costume jewelry on which the company had spent a lot of thought, time, and money. Three representatives of the company would be more impressive than two, and Joe wanted to be as impressive as possible on this occasion.

Charles Lyman welcomed them with what was by now his customary warmth. They all shook hands with him. They all sat down. They all chatted a few minutes. Eventually Lyman asked, "Well, boys, what have you got for me today?" Joe started presenting the trays. As Lyman examined each tray in silence, a frown began to grow on his face. Finally, he asked, "Who designed these for you, Joe? Gypsies?"

"How do you mean?" Joe asked.

Lyman shook his head. "Gaudy. Very gaudy, Joe. Too much." He shook his head again and moved back. "I can't use them, Joe. Women are looking for simple jewelry these days. Plain. Neat. This stuff looks like undergrowth from the Everglades."

The three Foster Grant hearts in the room stopped beating. All three men knew that a small fortune had already gone into the line and that, at this moment, the Foster Grant injection molding machines were turning out thousands of the parts which dozens of workers would be making into hundreds more pieces of the same design.

Harry Richards managed, "Charlie, can you give us any ideas?"

"Yes," Lyman said. "Get rid of most of the leaves, some of the petals and a few of the stems."

Joe said: "Thanks, Charlie. We'll get back to you."

"Any time, boys."

They left.

They did not talk as they left Lyman's office and went to the elevator. They did not talk on the ride to the ground. They did not talk as they left the building. But deep growls were beginning to emanate from Milt Bernstein. He saw a Woolworth store and said, "I'll be right back." In the store, he bought a couple of tubes of glue, a pair of scissors, pliers, and tweezers. When he rejoined Joe and Harry outside, they flagged a cab and rode in stormy silence to their hotel.

In the lobby, Milt said, "I've got some ideas for the jewelry. Can I have the sample case, Joe?" Joe gave it to him. Milt said, "You two might as well have dinner and go to the movies. This job may take me all night. I'll see you for breakfast."

In his room, Milt took off his coat and rolled up his shirt sleeves. He called room service for a sandwich and some coffee. He placed a tray of the new line on an end table. He laid out his Woolworth purchases. He went to work.

The job did indeed take him all night. It was two in the

morning before he got the hang of it. At dawn, he still had three trays to do. Around seven-thirty, he placed the last of the remodeled pieces on the dresser to dry. His unused bed was strewn with discarded plastic foliage. He was in the bathroom washing the glue off his hands when the telephone rang.

Harry Richards said, "Joe wants to know if we can come and take a look at the stuff."

"Sure. I'll leave the door unlocked, in case I'm in the shower."

Milt was just lathering up for his shave when Joe and Harry came in. Harry said, "Hey, Milt, it smells like a locker room in here."

"That's the glue," Milt said.

"Let's get some air." Harry opened the window. Then he joined Joe at the dresser to look at Milt's work. The new design was simple and plain and neat enough to be fit for a nun.

Milt came out of the bathroom. "What do you think, Joe?"

Joe shrugged. "Well, Milt, you sure stripped it."

Milt said, "I've got enough stuff on the bed to make two more complete sets."

Harry asked, "Are you sure this is what Charlie Lyman had in mind?"

"I did what he said. I got rid of most of the leaves, some of the petals, and a few of the stems."

"Looks kind of naked," Harry said.

Joe said: "Let's risk it. We've got to have a decision.

Remember, thousands of the old design will come off the assembly line in Leominster today, unless we stop them. We've got to let my father know."

Harry checked his watch. "It's too early to call Charlie Lyman for an appointment. Let's have breakfast. I'll call him exactly at nine."

Exactly at nine, Lyman told Harry he could see him exactly at nine-fifteen; otherwise, he was tied up for the day.

Quickly they packed Milt's creations into the display case, and Harry hurried away. For Joe and Milton, there could be nothing but the ordeal of waiting.

At ten, they had not heard from Harry.

At ten-thirty, they wondered if they should call Lyman to find out whether Harry ever got there.

At eleven, Milt finished his second pack of cigarettes. Joe badly wanted some coffee, but he didn't want to use the phone in case Harry called, got the busy signal, then disappeared again.

Harry's soft knock on the door came at eleven-twenty. Milt raced across the room and swung open the door. There stood Harry, sample case in hand, his face expressionless. He entered and crossed the room and placed the case on a chair, and then he turned and faced them.

Joe said, "F'God's sake, Harry, say something. How did it go?"

Harry said, "It went great."

Milt asked, "He took some stuff?"

Harry said, "He took the whole line."

Joe let loose a cheer, then rushed to the phone to call Sam.

Milt stepped forward to accept the applause.

Harry said, "Hold it, boys." They stopped and looked at him. He said, "Charlie Lyman took the whole line, all right. But he took the line he saw yesterday. He wants the original design."

Deep growls emanated from Milton Bernstein.

      ❋   ❋   ❋   ❋

So the team was shaping up. On the eve of World War II, people at Foster Grant used to say that the company stood on three pillars—Joe Foster as the boss, Harry Richards as vice president in charge of sales, and Roy Gettens as vice president in charge of production and shipping. Gettens was a remarkable man. A native of Leominster, he graduated from the local high school in 1923 and won a scholarship to Harvard. Family financial problems prevented him from taking it, and he went to work at Foster Grant. He began as a jewelry polisher, a job that was done by hand when he did it but which was eventually done by a machine he helped develop. Like everybody else at Foster Grant, Roy Gettens moved around the plant, learning this job and that one, until he could do just about every job in the place. Over the years, he moved up in authority and responsibility, and in 1941 he was vice president in charge of production and shipping.

Roy Gettens was an efficiency expert long before this type of work became a regular part of the business world. He carried around a little black book in which he listed the performance of every piece of equipment in the factory. Arriving at work at seven-fifteen every morning, he would go through the plant and discuss the previous day's performance with every supervisor. Any piece of equipment that fell below eighty-five percent efficiency was immediately shut down for repairs. Gettens felt it was better to do without a machine for a day or two than to run it at a loss. This settled, Gettens then gave the supervisors a production target for the day for every machine. The men knew that if anything went wrong during the day, Gettens was to be notified immediately so that he could make a decision.

In 1940, Leominster and Foster Grant were faced with a phenomenon new to them, labor unrest. Union organizers were entering Leominster in force, and a number of wildcat strikes had already taken place. Joe Foster realized that this was more than an incidental happening, that both his company and the community would have to adjust to this new trend in labor relations.

He called upon the New York law firm which represented Foster Grant and the Goodmans, and which still represents them, to assign one of its members experienced in labor relations to this task. Jack Chatkis was the man. He arrived in Leominster for what he thought would be a short assignment, but almost thirty years later he is still there, serving as the company's senior vice president as Foster Grant is celebrating its Golden Anniversary. In common with others in the company, he, too, moved from task to task and position to position, and he has been intimately involved in the growth and progress of the company.

The outbreak of World War II put new demands on everybody at Foster Grant. Overnight, sources of supply were cut off, jobs were frozen, and wages were frozen. Few companies in Leominster qualified for government contracts, so the town went dead at a time the rest of the country was gearing for wartime production. Not since Irene Castle's haircut had Leominster come to such a standstill. Even the Depression hadn't caused such havoc. Understandably, factory workers began appealing to the local Labor Board for permission to seek employment elsewhere; understandably, employers, pressed by payrolls that weren't returning any income, were torn between letting their people go and hanging on to them in hopes of a break.

The immediate crisis resulted from the failure of the general public to recognize the great value of plastics as a substitute material—and most of Leominster was engaged in producing plastic articles. The prospect that, if the war lasted any length of time, there would eventually be a shortage of rubber and metals did not seem to strike the men in charge of the country's war industries. Joe Foster certainly realized this, and it was the argument he took to the Leominster Chamber of Commerce and which the whole town then took on to Washington and to major industrial centers. Even so, it took almost two years for the shortages of rubber and metals to make themselves felt seriously enough and for top echelon to get the message about plastics. And then the pendulum swung the other way. Suddenly the government put fortunes into expanding the facilities of the major plastics manufacturers. Any company that could mold plastics had to struggle to get the powders and then struggle with production problems and then struggle with government specifications. Leominster got a different problem: besides the loss of men who had gone into the military, the town had lost a big slice of its labor force that had been authorized to move elsewhere during the lull, and now there weren't enough people around to do all the work. This was when and why Foster Grant and other local manufacturers turned to Fort Devens and the servicemen who could work part-time.

As the war wore on, more and more of the plastics and other chemicals which Foster Grant normally used in its processes became unavailable to it. There either just weren't enough to go around or some of the components were required for more important government matériels. Once again, the inventive and technical skills of Foster Grant's personnel were stretched to the utmost. No sooner would a suitable substitute be developed or found than that, too, would become unavailable. Looking back, it is now almost impossible to believe that in spite of all these difficulties with materials and with equipment which was running twenty-four hours a day, seven days a week, on war production, the company still managed to maintain its delivery schédules to the various branches of the armed services and did a substantial amount of subcontracting for other major suppliers to the government.

The company quickly reached a point where eighty percent of its production was for the military. Joe Foster, Harry Richards, and Milt Bernstein made most of the contacts with the military, in the Boston area, New York, and Washington, sometimes taking along their own ideas but usually tracking down military needs which Foster Grant could meet. Jack Chatkis handled the actual contracts, and it was up to Roy Gettens to see that the articles were properly made. The articles included goggles for ski troops, the eyepiece and nozzle for gas masks, and parts for submarines being built at Groton and New London in Connecticut. An article Foster Grant made by the millions was a transparent visor used for face protection by desert fighters in North Africa. Years later, Joe Foster saw a movie on the Sahara combat and the actors were wearing Foster Grant visors which had somehow found their way into a Hollywood prop room. Another unique Foster Grant item that followed American military men all over the world was a plastic match box, with a compass on the lid, and waxed matches that could practically be lighted under water. As always, necessity was the mother of Foster Grant inventions.

Foster Grant also did war work for other companies which had items that required molding that the companies could not do themselves. This area was handled mostly by Bill Lane, a Leominster High School star athlete who had joined Foster Grant sales before the war. One of the most important contracts Lane brought in was with the Gillette Company.

When the war was over, Gillette, having learned of the advantages of plastics, decided to replace its paper packaging of blades by a more utilitarian and beautiful plastic package. Many serious problems were presented by this apparently simple task. The packaging of the millions of Gillette blades is highly automated. The slightest variation in thickness of the packaging material would jam the packaging machinery and cause critical delays. It took many months of design and subsequent field application on the part of engineers from Gillette and Foster Grant to work out a plastic package which would meet these problems. For years thereafter, Foster Grant was the only company that could maintain the close tolerances required. With this new package came the demand for various types of plastic boxes to house the Gillette razors and blades, and Foster Grant produced these, too. In the Golden Anniversary, Gillette and Foster Grant were still working together, and the latter is very proud of the part it played in the development of the popular Techmatic Gillette razor.

The end of the war brought Foster Grant numerous citations for excellence from various departments of the military. And the end of the war finally gave Foster Grant a chance to make some important improvements in the plant. The fact that the company's pre-war machinery had withstood the tremendous demands of wartime production, operating around the clock for two years without collapsing, which was slightly less than miraculous, was high tribute to the skills of the Foster Grant engineers and mechanics. Now the opportunity had arrived for new machinery and new techniques, most of them developed within the company itself.

Moreover, there had been two developments which gave Foster Grant high hopes for a greater and a diversified future. First, sunglasses had become a fashion item. Claire McCardle, a famous couturiere, had introduced her own designs for sunglasses to go with summer outfits and thereby set a trend. Miss McCardle's far-out designs were executed by the American Optical Company and sold for around fifteen dollars a pair, which limited their market. Encouraged by this trend, Foster Grant designers went far out—to a harlequin design, to rhinestones, to different colored lenses—and injection molding enabled the company to produce lines of high-fashion sunglasses that sold for as little as a quarter.

And this: wartime demands for plastic articles had led the U.S. government to subsidize expansion of facilities by most of the leaders in the chemical industry. Before the war, Union Carbide and Dow were producing polystyrene; during the war, Monsanto, Koppers, and others went into the styrenes. It had been the limited pre-war supply of polystyrene which had curbed Foster Grant production. Now, with resin production so greatly increased, the Foster Grant horizon became unlimited. The post-war challenge was simply a matter of finding company outlets for the company's output, and this meant expanding the company's sales force.

In 1945, Joe Watkins was brought into the New York office. Before the war, Joe Watkins had been with Kresge, which gave him experience in the syndicate field. During the war, he worked with U.S. Maritime Commission. Joe Watkins had gone to school with Harry Richards' wife, so there was already a friendship between the two men when Richards invited Watkins to join Foster Grant as his assistant. Besides calling on wholesalers across the country, Milt Bernstein was also making contact with sales representatives. After the war, other U.S. companies went into sunglasses, and sunglasses were being imported from Italy, Germany, France, and Japan. Because of this sudden rash of competition, Foster Grant at first could not always sign with the best sales representatives in a given area, but Joe Foster advised Bernstein, "For now, get the best you can. Later on, we'll get the best there is."

During this period of growth, the New York office had a series of homes. When the Goodmans moved to Jersey City, Foster Grant went with them, but this soon proved to be inconvenient for New York calls. The office moved back to the city, first to Varick Street, then for several years to 34th Street opposite Macy's, and in 1956 to the Empire State Building, where it remained. By the Golden Anniversary Year, Foster Grant had its own sales staff permanently established in Miami, Atlanta, Dallas, Cleveland, Chicago, and Los Angeles, with the best representation available in other major cities. There were, in 1969, approximately eighty salesmen covering the country for Foster Grant, with about thirty of them being on the company staff. Together, they had acquired over a hundred thousand outlets for Foster Grant sunglasses and, in terms of volume, had made Foster Grant the country's leading manufacturer of sunglasses.

Early in 1953, a double tragedy struck Foster Grant. Harry Richards, returning from a road trip, had landed at the Newark airport, where he had left his car. It was never established how the heartbreaking accident occurred, but while he was driving to his home at Morristown, New Jersey, his car left the road, crashed, and Harry Richards was killed. At approximately the same time, Roy Gettens became ill and was hospitalized; doctors discovered an inoperable cancer; Roy Gettens died on March 17.

Joe Foster felt the two losses profoundly. Not only had he suddenly lost two close friends within a month, but he also lost the two men on whom he had relied so heavily for years in running the company. Joe Foster told Chatkis, "I can't go on, Jack. I'll never find anybody to replace Harry and Roy. I'm going to sell out."

Chatkis said, "You have to go on, Joe, and you know it. This company is your family. It's your life."

To replace Harry Richards and Roy Gettens was impossible, but an effort had to be made to fill the great void caused by the loss of them. Milt Bernstein succeeded Harry Richards as head of sales. Joe Watkins took over in New York, with Lou Jones as his assistant. Jack Chatkis took charge of production, with Bunny McDowell running the shipping department.

And this has happened: Roy Gettens' son—Bill—had gone to work for Foster Grant in 1946, after finishing at the Cushing Academy. Like his father, Bill Gettens worked in many departments of production and management. In the Golden Anniversary Year, he was the company's director of purchasing. At the time of Harry Richards' death, his son— Harry, Jr.—was a student at the University of Pennsylvania. In 1955, Harry Richards, Jr., joined the sales force at Foster Grant. By the Golden Anniversary Year, he was Milt Bernstein's assistant, handling wholesalers and brokers across the country.

Jack Chatkis had been right. The company was Joe Foster's family and his life. But then Foster Grant became a family and a life for many other people, as well.

* * * *

Like the good missionaries that good salesmen should be, the Foster Grant salesmen never missed a chance to spread the faith. Zeal was demonstrated at every level mainly because it was a way of life at the top. Sales figures never fascinated Joe Foster as much as the details on how an important sale was brought about. As administrative responsibilities tied him increasingly to a desk, his favorite moments were at sales conferences when he could gather at a bar with the men and listen to their experiences with this item or that item with this buyer or that buyer. Usually the stories had one point in common: the sale had made been because of the salesman's enthusiasm for the product. Often the conversation would turn to the products, and the men would explain why they felt this item was doing so well or how to make some other item do better. Out of this could come ideas for new products.

Joe Watkins proved to be a good example of the dedicated salesman. Working with chain variety stores, he had only to walk two blocks in any direction from his hotels on the road to find out how Foster Grants were doing in the stores. Of course, the main office sent him the figures regularly, but he had learned that he could pick up important information by listening to the conversations while people made their choices. It was from these eavesdropping tours of his that Joe Watkins discerned the growing preference by women for sunglasses which provided eye protection without hiding the natural beauty of their eyes and the added beauty of their eye makeup. Foster Grant began making sunglasses with larger frames and with lenses tinted pink, pale blue, and various pastels. Then false eyelashes became popular. Women were overheard to complain that when their eyes blinked in the normal way they had to take off their sunglasses to get their eyes open again. Foster Grant began making sunglasses with a well-defined convex lens which allowed women to flutter their false eyelashes and still be able to see. One day the new lens enabled Joe Watkins to give personal assistance to a damsel in distress. Leaving the office, he had taken his sample case with him on the trip home because he was going directly to the airport in the morning to begin another road trip. On the subway, he noticed that the young lady sitting opposite him was having the familiar problem with her false eyelashes behind a pair of sunglasses made by a competitor. Joe took a pair of the new line out of his case, stepped to the girl, and said, "Excuse me, miss. I'm not being fresh, but I've noticed the trouble you're having with those sunglasses. Will you please accept this pair as a gift? They're Foster Grants, and I'm with the company. Tell your friends." The surprised woman accepted the sunglasses with a nod, removed the old glasses and donned the Foster Grants, and for the rest of their ride together she kept fluttering her gratitude across the aisle at Joe.

Probably the greatest test of company loyalty ever put to Joe Watkins occurred during the five-year run of *My Fair Lady*. It was only natural that when an out-of-town buyer headed for New York he should call upon his friend Joe Watkins to get him a couple of tickets for the smash hit. And it was only natural that Joe Watkins should want to spend the evening with his friend the out-of-town buyer, first at dinner and then at the theater. Joe later recalled, "After I saw *My Fair Lady* fourteen times, I couldn't take it any more. From then on, I'd have dinner with a buyer and his wife, then I'd hand them the two tickets and I'd tell them I'd see them later at their hotel. I sure was glad when that show finally closed. I was spending so much time hanging around lobbies that every hotel detective in New York had me listed as a suspicious character."

For Milton Bernstein, company loyalty was a matter of sheer determination. He traveled constantly, and he spoke about his products with such enthusiasm that throughout the merchandising world he soon became known as "Mr. Sunglasses." It was beyond Milt Bernstein how any buyer could take a look at Foster Grant sunglasses and still prefer another brand, and this was the sort of challenge that drove Milt to extremes.

Around 1956, Milt Bernstein made up his mind that he was going to place Foster Grants in every Rexall drugstore in the country, and the company's structure provided his main obstacles. Rexall outlets fell into three categories: 1) stores completely owned by Rexall, 2) stores partly owned by Rexall, and 3) independently-owned stores that carried Rexall products. At the time, Rexall carried its own brand of sunglasses, produced by another manufacturer. By then, Foster Grant rated second in terms of volume among the country's sunglass manufacturers and, probably, first in terms of product quality. The company supplying Rexall rated tenth or eleventh in volume and, in Milt Bernstein's opinion, the company didn't rate at all.

Milt Bernstein made several trips to Los Angeles for the express purpose of converting the Rexall buyer to Foster Grants, but he got nowhere. The buyer simply said he was satisfied with the sunglasses the company already had and saw no reason for making a change. Milt would have settled for a chance to compete, but he could not get it at the top level. So he decided to take the hard road. On another cross-country trip, he called on Rexall outlets which either were only partly owned by the parent organization or were independents, and he persuaded twenty-five managers to place a Foster Grant carrousel next to the display of the Rexall brand. At the end of the season, every manager reported an increase in sunglass sales, ranging from six hundred fifty dollars to fifteen hundred dollars over the previous year, and in each store the increase was attributable to the sale of Foster Grants.

Armed with this exciting ammunition, Milt sat down at his desk in Leominster and wrote a letter to John Bowles, then president of Rexall. Milt first cited the comparative sales figures, noting that he was enclosing a detailed list, store by store, and then he said, "Mr. Bowles, I invite you to choose any six Rexall stores where Foster Grant can place a display of our products. If at the end of the season any one of the stores fails to report an increase in the sale of sunglasses, and if in any of the stores Foster Grant fails to outsell its competitors, your company can keep the entire supply without charge."

Four days after Milton Bernstein mailed his letter to John Bowles in Los Angeles, his telephone rang a few minutes past nine. It was Joe Foster, who said, "Milt, I just got a call from John Bowles, at Rexall. He likes your idea of the test in six stores. He gave me the list. I'll send it over to you. Milt, this is a great chance for us."

Milt Bernstein had the right to be elated, but while listening to Joe he had glanced at his watch, so he asked, "Where did he call from, Joe?"

Joe said, "From his office in Los Angeles, of course."

Milt said, "Good Lord, Joe, it's six o'clock in the morning out there. That guy works harder than you!"

A year later, Foster Grant sunglasses were in every Rexall outlet in the chain.

❀   ❀   ❀   ❀

Joe Foster did indeed work hard, hence this memo:

"It has been brought to the attention of the management of Foster Grant that executives and department heads of the company have been coming into the office on weekends to finish business they were unable to complete during our regular workweek. As much as such loyalty and dedication are appreciated, the management feels this practice should be ended. A man's family has a right to his time and attention on weekends. Furthermore, the rules of physical and mental health require a man to have time away from his job for his hobbies and the athletic activities that will take him out-doors intó our excellent New England climate and fresh air. Therefore, the management of Foster Grant wishes to make this point specifically clear: No executive or department head in the company shall be expected to put in any more than our normal sixty-hour week."

7

The name of Foster Grant as the world's leading brand of sunglasses was common knowledge in the company's Golden Anniversary Year of 1969, but many people didn't realize that other Foster Grant products were also entering their homes in countless shapes and sizes. These were products made by other manufacturers from Foster Grant plastics. The company's cautious entry into the field of petrochemistry fifteen years earlier had turned out to be the Cinderella story of the industry. Adhering to Joe Foster's principle of starting small and building as the market grew, the Foster Grant Chemicals Division began as an internal department to meet the company's own needs. But as a market appeared and grew, so did production. Then, in May 1954, new facilities dedicated in Louisiana put Foster Grant into the realm of the giants.

Foster Grant went into the production of plastic resins as a means of survival. A great deal of thought went into the decision. Production headaches accumulated over a period of thirty years certainly influenced the final decision. So did the plain fact of technological progress. So did competition. So did the state of the plastics industry itself.

Actually, the company had been moving in the direction of plastics production for a long time. Even before injection molding, Foster Grant was compounding its own plastic substances from cellulose acetate flakes for the sake of quality control, and injection molding made quality control a matter of even greater importance. The development of injection molding by Foster Grant achieved for plastics what the invention of the carburetor by Gottlieb Daimler achieved for motorized transportation. Both the plastics industry and the auto industry would have remained stumbling infants for years longer if others had not shown them how to make better use of what they already had. With injection molding machines, it was Sam Foster who showed the way. With plastics, it was Joe Foster.

In both instances, success was achieved because neither father nor son would take no for an answer.

After World War II, giants like Dow, Monsanto, and Union Carbide expanded their plants and became even bigger giants. At the same time, Foster Grant was growing bigger, and so were the company's needs for polystyrene. By 1948, Foster Grant was the biggest user of polystyrene in the world and the world's largest fabricator of injection-molded articles.

And Foster Grant had no control over its sources of supply. Joe Foster couldn't stop worrying about this. He knew that at any moment his supply could be shut off for any number of reasons, and this was no way to run a business. Another area of concern was quality control. Foster Grant was buying a general-purpose polystyrene, which usually arrived in the form of colorless granules. In order to make better products, the company processed the substance with rubber, resulting in an impact material which could turn out articles that were stronger, more durable, and more resistant to heat and rough treatment than regular polystyrene. By now, Foster Grant also had its own color laboratory, which could reproduce every color in the rainbow, and the coloring was introduced during the impact processing. As satisfactory as the end product was, it could have been better if the rubber were introduced earlier, during polymerization, with higher quality control assured in every batch.

And another area of concern was cost. Foster Grant was then paying thirty cents a pound for the general-purpose polystyrene. Besides being the biggest buyer of the resin, Foster Grant also paid its bills on receipt. Joe Foster felt that these two circumstances warranted a small discount from the chemical producers. The chemical producers did not agree.

Something had to be done. When, therefore, in 1949 a

chemist by the name of Elmer Derby, with styrene polymerization knowledge, became available, he was given a hearty welcome. A pilot plant kettle was installed in a small building adjacent to the main plant at Leominster, a quantity of the monomer was obtained, and in short order Foster Grant was turning out its own brand of the resin. This event changed the company's chemical needs from the polymer to the monomer of styrene, and this was not welcome news to the industry. Only two companies—Monsanto and Koppers—were willing to sell the monomer. Others felt they were simply inviting competition in the polymer field by selling the more basic compound to somebody who had the equipment to go into their business. At first, Foster Grant had no intention of marketing its resin. The whole idea had been to guarantee the company's own source of supply. After a great deal of discussion, it was Koppers that finally became the major provider of the monomer to Foster Grant. Two production-size kettles were installed, and by summer 1950 Foster Grant was producing enough polystyrene for its own use, with some left over for another Leominster molder.

Then, in June 1950, the Korean conflict broke out. Once again, the giants of the chemical industry were put into wartime production. Resins were again rationed. Had Foster Grant not gone into its own polymer production, the company would have faced a standstill for three years. Even though the Koppers allotment became limited, it at least was not cut off, and Foster Grant was able to hold its own in both civilian and war production.

But once again something definitely had to be done. Just as Foster Grant could not risk a shortage of the polymer, it could not risk a long-term shortage of the monomer. It seemed to Joe Foster that the only real protection the company could acquire was to go into the production of the monomer as well. Joe foresaw that in another two or three years the Foster Grant need for polystyrene would reach ten million pounds a year, and his original intention was to build a monomer facility to produce that amount of the primary material. In the opinion of the industry, however, this was a joke. Experience had convinced the experts that the chemistry of monomer-making was so complex that it could not be made in such small quantities. As far as Joe Foster was concerned, the experts had been wrong before and they could be wrong again.

Joe Foster talked to Derby about the possibility of building a small monomer facility. Derby said he did not feel qualified to advise Joe on matters involving construction, but he had a friend, John Debell, a chemical engineer and a partner in Debell and Richardson, consultants, in Connecticut, who might be helpful. Debell had done some work in Germany on monomer production and probably could give Joe the information he needed. A telephone conference was arranged; Elmer Derby introduced Joe Foster and John Debell, and then Joe explained what he had in mind. Debell asked for some time to think about it. A week later, he was in Leominster.

Joe Foster took an immediate liking to John Debell. The man was informed, specific, forthright, direct. They were quickly on a first-name basis. But Joe did not like what John Debell had to tell him.

Debell said, "I've calculated this from every angle, Joe,

and the smallest monomer plant I can envision would have to have an annual capacity of forty million pounds. And you'd need seven to eight million dollars to build it."

Joe Foster shook his head. "It'll be years before Foster Grant can use forty million pounds a year of anything. What would I do with the leftover in the meantime?"

Debell shrugged. "You've already got your own polymerization set up. Put in a few more kettles, polymerize your entire monomer production, and market what you don't need yourself."

"I suppose we could do that," Joe conceded. "But we've got another problem first. Where do we get the seven or eight million dollars? We don't have money like that. And I doubt that a bank would lend it to us."

"You've got an even more basic problem than that," said Debell. "We're in a war. There's a gasoline shortage, and that means there's a benzene shortage. And if you don't have benzene, you can't get the monomer in the first place."

"So what do we do ?"

"Why don't you wait until after the war?"

"Who knows when that's going to be?" Joe settled back in his chair. "I hate the idea of an uncertain time lag. Isn't there some way we can get this thing going?"

"As far as the benzene is concerned, maybe," said Debell. "You can use benzol. Europeans use it instead of gasoline to run their cars. If you can get some benzol, you can get started. And if you get the benzol before you get your plant, maybe one of the Big Boys will do your processing for you."

"Koppers might," Joe suggested. "Will you look into the benzol deal for me? I've got something else I've got to check."

He wanted to check with the Goodmans. As partners in Foster Grant, they would be involved in any indebtedness the company would have to incur to build an expensive chemical facility, and so Joe felt they had the right to be consulted as well as the right to oppose the move before he went too far with it. Joe went to New Jersey and laid his plan before the Goodmans, including the marketing of the surplus resins at least temporarily.

Abe Goodman frowned a little. "Why, Joe?" he asked. "Why do you want to go into that? You'd have to go out and fight the giants—Dow and Monsanto and Carbide. That is no place for Foster Grant."

Joe asked, "Would it be so bad to be in the same family with General Motors?"

Abe thought about it. "No, Joe, it wouldn't. All right. Look into it, Joe. Maybe we can manage it."

The benzol deal turned out to be unexpectedly complicated. Joe Foster and John Debell had to make four trips to Belgium and France to negotiate terms. The European refiners were willing to sell their benzol—but not for cash. They wanted American gasoline in exchange, at a rate of three gallons of benzol for one gallon of gas. Because of the wartime controls, Joe Foster had to get approval from Washington to send gasoline out of the country. Even then, something went wrong. A boatload of benzol left Europe but somehow got detoured on the high seas. Joe found out later that part of the cargo landed in the warehouse of one of the U.S. giants. There was a flurry of angry letters and telephone calls, but to no avail.

And yet some good came out of the venture. On their

last trip to Europe, Joe Foster and John Debell went to Germany to visit the company where Debell had previously worked on the monomer. The Germans did not laugh at Joe's plans for a small annual output of the monomer. In fact, they thought Debell's calculations of forty million pounds were unnecessarily high, and they told the two Americans about another Germany company that had figured a way to produce as little as eighteen million pounds a year. Joe Foster and John Debell went to inspect this company, and what they saw was amazing. The small company was operating in part of a building that had been bombed during World War II, and even the operable part was being held together by wire and rubber bands. But the company was doing the job. For Joe Foster, this was a great relief. For John Debell, it was an eye-opener. When Joe said he'd prefer an even smaller annual output, the Germans were confident it could be done. They offered to send their own engineers to America as advisers in case Foster Grant ran into any problems. Meanwhile, they accorded Debell free range of their plant.

By the time Joe Foster and John Debell returned to New York, Debell had revised his calculations and now proposed a plant with a capacity of twelve million pounds of monomer a year and costing between three and four million dollars. He also estimated that production of the monomer would cost fourteen cents a pound, which was four or five cents higher than had been anticipated. But then, Foster Grant was already paying twenty-one cents a pound for the monomer the company was buying, so in the long run there would be a good saving.

A lot remained to be done. It was now early summer,

1953. The fighting in Korea had stopped, and truce negotiations were going on. Government controls on oil had eased and benzene was becoming available. Having decided to proceed, Joe Foster had to move in three directions. First, there was the matter of a loan of almost four million dollars; second, selecting the best location for the new plant; third, being licensed under the prevailing patented processes for producing monomer, or developing a process not yet patented. And Joe Foster proceeded in the three directions at once.

—He felt he would have a better chance of getting the loan from insurance companies, rather than from banks, so he sent out feelers in that area. He knew that a favorable decision on the loan would be based on more than Foster Grant as a going concern. He would have to prove that his plan for a small monomer plant was feasible. As his staff began to prepare a convincing presentation, Debell and Richardson went to work on blueprints for the facility.

—Obviously, the plant would have to be near its source of ethylene, which meant an oil refinery. This probably meant somewhere in Texas. Joe Foster had no contacts in the Texas oil industry, but through a mutual friend, he was put in touch with Dr. Robert E. Purvin, a young consulting engineer just starting his own business in Dallas. Though Purvin had no experience in monomers, he knew oil, he knew oil people, and he knew Texas.

Joe Foster went to Dallas to meet Purvin. Here again was another case of instant friendship. A Texan, Bob Purvin was a tall, well-built man, pleasant, outgoing, always in good spirits. Looking back during the Golden Anniversary Year,

Purvin said, "I had a reason for being in good spirits with Joe Foster. Besides liking him, I knew that he was saving my life. I had just started my own business; my fee was a hundred dollars a day, but it was a rare day when I earned it. I needed Joe as a client. His friendship was an unexpected bonus."

They spent a few days driving around Texas looking for a plant site, and they agreed that if they found nothing during Joe's limited stay, Purvin would continue the search on his own. One day they stopped for lunch in a drugstore, and as they were heading back to Purvin's car Bob stopped to look at the store's window display of electric alarm clocks. He said, "I'll have to get one of those."

"An alarm clock?" Joe asked.

"Yes. I have a helluva time getting up in the morning," Purvin admitted. "When I'm home, my wife manages to get me up. But if I'm going to be spending time on the road for you, I'll need one of those things."

Joe said, "Just a minute." He went into the store; he was soon back to Purvin and handed him a package. "Here's your alarm clock."

The clock probably cost fifteen dollars—a lot of money to Bob Purvin in those days—and he said, "Joe, you didn't have to do this."

"Oh, yes, I did," said Joe. "You're working for Foster Grant now, and at a hundred dollars a day I don't want you sleeping late on company time."

The day would come when Bob Purvin's fee would be a thousand dollars a day, and he always traveled with Joe Foster's fifteen-dollar clock.

Bob Purvin arranged a meeting for Joe Foster with the Gulf Oil Corporation, out of which came the agreement that Gulf would supply the ethylene to Foster Grant from one of its Texas refineries. Gulf was then reverting to civilian production; the Foster Grant account would require some expansion, and so a delivery date of several months later was agreed upon.

Joe Foster also commissioned Bob Purvin to locate a man experienced in monomer production. Purvin knew Dr. Drew Mayfield, then working in Texas for the Celanese Corporation. Mayfield had acquired his monomer experience previously at Dow. As much as Drew Mayfield wanted to go to work for Foster Grant, he questioned the propriety of joining Foster Grant because of his previous association with Dow. He therefore went to the Dow management, told them about the Foster Grant offer, and stated that he would take the job only if Dow approved. Mayfield's highly ethical position impressed the Dow people; they told him to go ahead. During the conversation, someone asked about the Foster Grant plans, and when Mayfield mentioned the twelve million pounds a year, there was laughter from the Dow staff, as though Foster Grant were building a toy.

The Gulf refinery was located in Orange, Texas. The town had a good Chamber of Commerce interested in industrial development and eager to cooperate with new companies. Shipping facilities were good, and experienced labor was available. Bob Purvin agreed to supervise construction. These matters settled, Joe Foster returned to Leominster.

And he returned to a headache. All the necessary documentation had been submitted to the New England insurance company that had expressed interest in lending the building funds to Foster Grant. There had been several conferences. Everything seemed to be going all right. Then an executive for the insurance company asked for another conference.

And he said, "Mr. Foster, we don't in the least doubt your ability to run this new venture. But we don't know anything about the styrene industry, and so we have consulted with some people in petrochemicals. They feel that such a small plant can't possibly be operated at the cost you cite. They say you'll go broke in less than two years."

"Who said that?" Joe asked.

"I'm sorry, but the consultations were confidential," said the man. "But I can tell you they were people in the industry."

"You wouldn't expect competitors to give us their best wishes, would you?"

"I am aware of that," the man said. "That's why I have a proposal to put to you. Would you accept the appraisal of a qualified expert who is not in the industry?"

"Yes," said Joe, "provided he will listen to both sides."

"Of course."

They agreed on a professor of petrochemistry at a Pennsylvania university. All of the Foster Grant documentation was submitted to him. His opinion: it wouldn't work. As far as the insurance company was concerned, that settled the question of the loan. The reaction at Foster Grant was sheer anguish. If Joe Foster hadn't seen the German operation with his own eyes, he would have accepted the professor's opinion, but he knew the visit to the German plant had not been a dream, and so he was ready to fight back.

A conference call was arranged with Bob Purvin, Drew

Mayfield, and John Debell, and Joe said, "Go see that guy. If you can't convince him that we're right in his own office, put him on a plane and take him to Germany."

The three engineers converged on the professor. They went over the documentation with him again and again; they drew diagrams of the production procedure; they showed him the German statistics; they offered him the trip. It was a case of the students teaching the teacher. As difficult as it must have been for the professor to reverse his professional opinion, he nevertheless did so. He wrote the insurance company that, in light of additional information brought to his attention, the Foster Grant project was indeed feasible. The loan was granted.

But troubles were not over. First, as construction was about to start, Gulf Oil notified Joe Foster that it would be unable to start supplying the ethylene on time and that it could not give a definite date when shipments could begin. Bob Purvin and his alarm clock hit the road again. He was able to get a definite commitment from the Esso refinery at Baton Rouge, Louisiana. Adjacent to the refinery was available land, not only for the contemplated small plant, but for all foreseeable expansion.

But there was a period in 1953 when it looked as though Foster Grant would have to use the land to grow cotton. The major chemical companies turned down all offers by Foster Grant for the use of their monomer process patents.

＊　＊　＊　＊

Bob Purvin said, "Well, Joe, you have two choices: either drop the whole thing, or we invent our own process."

Joe said, "Please, this is no time for jokes."

"It's no joke," said Purvin.

"There's no choice, either," said Joe.

"You're going to quit?"

"You know any inventors?"

"I can look around."

He did not look far. He started with himself.

He and his assistant, Cliff Shaw, and Drew Mayfield began to burn the midnight oil for weeks and months, and then finally he was able to tell Joe, "We believe we have a process that won't infringe."

Joe Foster asked, "If it works, can we patent it?"

Purvin said, "Yes."

Joe said, "Go ahead, then."

Harry E. Bovay, head of a mechanical engineering firm in Houston, was a friend of Purvin's and was called in to make the new unit. The project was classified as even more Top Secret than the injection molding machines in the Mystery Room on Lancaster Street, and for similar reasons: if it worked, fine; if it didn't, nobody would know.

Then came the day for the crucial test.

It worked like a charm.

The process was awarded a patent in the United States and in the other principal industrial countries.

Construction proceeded on the facility at Baton Rouge. In May 1954 the Foster Grant monomer plant, the fifth such plant in the country, came on stream. In the first year, production was held at a million pounds a month—twelve million pounds for the year, as planned. The second year, production was planned for twenty-four million pounds, but the operation was going so smoothly that the year's output reached thirty million. Ten years later, in 1964, the plant was turning out two hundred twenty million pounds annually. By May 1969, the Golden Anniversary Month, the Baton Rouge facility had produced two billion one hundred million pounds of monomer—and it was still growing.

Most of the Baton Rouge production was being used at Leominster for Foster Grant's own purposes. Logistics for the long journey were put to Charles Loiselle, who had worked part-time at Foster Grant while a cooperative student at Northeast University and then joined the company after his graduation in 1938. He arranged to have the monomer shipped by barge from Baton Rouge up the Mississippi and Ohio rivers to Pittsburgh. There the monomer was transferred to tank cars for the overland trip by rail to the siding which had been installed at the main plant at Leominster.

Of necessity, the polymerization facility at Leominster was enlarged, both to meet company needs and to fill the orders from other molders. Foster Grant's first resin was called Fostarene. It was a general-purpose resin which took color excellently and was immediately popular throughout the industry. At first, however, other molders were unreceptive when Joe Foster arrived to sell them the Foster Grant polystyrene. To a man, they said, "You're our competitor as a molder. Why should we want to buy your resin?"

And Joe would point out, "As a molder, I know the kind of molding materials you need. If you buy them from me, you will have free access to all the molding and marketing techniques my company has developed over the years."

It soon became clear to Joe Foster that building a company staff of resins salesmen was going to take time. With production going so well, he decided to turn to an established sales outlet to get on the market quickly, and the outlet he chose was H. Muehlstein and Company of New York. H. Muehlstein represented plastics and rubber producers from around the world, and over a period of fifty years, the company had earned a reputation of worldwide leadership and respect. Before Foster Grant began to produce its own plastics, it did a lot of buying from Muehlstein. Now, H. Muehlstein was selling for Foster Grant, and from the start this was a good arrangement for both companies.

In Foster Grant's Golden Anniversary Year, Al Chester, its president, said this:

"I rate Joe Foster among the most capable businessmen in the country. He is a realistic man, he always knows what he's doing, and he's got a lot of courage. Like any big business, the plastics industry is no place for boy scouts. In plastics, Foster Grant started at zero, and the leaders of the industry expected the company to stay there. By coming to H. Muehlstein, Foster Grant received the benefits of our many years in business and our thousands of contacts. We were able to open a lot of doors for Foster Grant in a hurry. On the other hand, the Muehlstein company derived the benefit of being the exclusive sales representative for excellent products being put out by a small company that was already internally geared for fast growth. It didn't take long for the giants of the plastics industry to stop laughing at the little upstart from Leominster because it didn't take long for that little upstart to turn into a giant itself."

But Foster Grant had something special going. As the company began to permeate the plastics industry in the late

1950s, Foster Grant already had behind it over thirty years of experience at molding. Some of the old-timers with the company had gone to work as boys on the country's first injection molding machines, and these natural, gifted, skillful mechanics became the company's servicemen to its plastics customers.

Like all machines, molding machines could have bad days, and it was not uncommon for the men and women operating these machines to blame the bad days on the plastic. This meant that the company which made the plastic had to send somebody to solve the problem. Other companies were sending specialists in plastics. Foster Grant was sending specialists in machines. As molders began to see the differences in the results, they preferred to do business with Foster Grant because of this extra and valuable service which they couldn't get anywhere else.

Besides being expert mechanics, these men also had to be expert diplomats. Jack Iacoboni, who went to work at Foster Grant in 1934, started going on the road for the company as a serviceman in 1955, and before his first trip Joe Foster told him, "Be honest with people. Speak their language. Be on their side."

Jack Iacoboni learned this: "I soon found out that a person who operates the same machine every day gets emotionally involved with it, and when the machine breaks down or turns out inferior work, it's like having a sickness in the family. I could understand this because I feel the same way about machinery myself. Obviously, the operator isn't going to take any of the blame if his machine acts up, and yet he can't believe that the machine he loves has turned against him. So the plastic gets blamed; and if the operator complains enough, it isn't unlikely that the company will change brands.

"So I had to develop a real bedside manner. For me, the operator was the important person, and I saw to it that he took part in any conversations I had with the foreman. I'd find out his first name. I'd ask him about his family. If his people came from Italy, I'd try some of my lousy Italian on him, just to give him a laugh and win his confidence. If the operator was a woman, I'd ask her about her kids, and if she had any teenagers, I'd say I didn't believe her because she didn't look old enough to have kids that age.

"And I'd let the plastics take the blame when we finally got around to discussing the symptoms. Generally, the problem was in the machine. Sometimes the management would send in its plastics man and he'd throw big words at me, so I had to get that language down, too. Now they don't trip me up any more. But when you are working in molding, all the scientific theories in the world won't help you. You can't go by the book. You've got to know machines."

People like Jack Iaconi can make a company great. A lot of people like him had turned the little upstart at Leominster into a giant in just a dozen years. And there was impressive evidence of this. In 1952, Joe Foster, the Goodmans, and their advisers literally went through hell to borrow the four million dollars to build the Baton Rouge facility, and they almost didn't make it. In 1968, Joe Foster, the Goodmans, and their board decided to take a real giant step by increasing the Baton Rouge capacity from two hundred fifty million pounds a year to seven hundred million.

Engineers estimated that the expansion would cost sixteen million dollars, which the company would have to borrow. This time the money was readily available.

8

In the Golden Anniversary Year, Grace Goodale, the first employee hired by Sam Foster in 1919, could remember this:

"In the old days, it was unusual for a small company in this town to give employees vacations with pay, but from the start Sam Foster gave us a week with pay. I remember when my first vacation came along. On my last day, Sam came around with the pay envelopes, as he always did, and he gave me my salary and the vacation money and told me to have a good time. Later, when I went into the office to say good-bye to him, Sam handed me a five-dollar gold piece and said, 'Grace, buy yourself a hat.' It was almost as much as I was earning a week."

And Grace Goodale would remember this:

"I always wanted a home of my own, and finally I found one that I really liked. But I wasn't sure that I could keep up the payments. It was a big house, and I wondered if it might be too much for me. I guess I talked about it around the plant quite a bit. One day, Sam said to me, "Grace, take the house. If it turns out to be too much for you, either in the size of the payments or the size of the place, I'll buy it from you and we'll work something out.' So I went ahead with it and everything worked out. Thanks to Sam Foster, I was eventually able to retire in a house of my own, paid for. Sam was always doing things like that for people."

He was. Sam Foster was probably the easiest touch in the world, and he never waited to be asked. He used to say, "Money problems are the easiest ones to solve." He knew, from his own experience, that this was not always true, but he always did what he could to help others solve theirs. Nobody will ever know the extent of such help—how often he paid somebody's rent or mortgage or hospital costs or grocery bill, sometimes knowing he would never see the money again. Being thanked embarrassed Sam. When anyone in his debt would approach him in obviously apologetic discomfort, Sam would stop him with, "Please. Have I mentioned it? Don't you."

Like father, like son.

One evening in 1968, Joe Foster was attending the annual dinner of the Foster Grant Twenty-five-Year Club,* of which he was a member, and he was called upon to say a few words. He talked about the company, which had been so much a part of the lives of everybody in the room. Things had changed a great deal. The company was no longer just Leominster-based but had spread out across the country. It had also spread out into new areas of production and would undoubtedly continue to do so. But one thing had not changed—the sense of family which had held the company together through so many changes. In a way, this was natural. Most of the people in the room had been born and raised in Leominster and had gone to the same schools and the same churches before going to work for the same company. Many of them had married someone else who worked at Foster Grant, and they, in turn, sent their children to the same schools and the same churches with children of other Foster Grant employees, and some of the children went to work at Foster Grant. A sense of family would be almost inevitable in those circumstances. There were exceptions, too. Present in the room were men and women who came to Foster Grant from other communities, people who were either brought in for some special job or who had decided for themselves that Leominster was where they wanted to live and Foster Grant was where they wanted to work. These people, too, had become family, and this would not have happened unless the family spirit was already in the company to assimilate them. The creative and productive atmosphere of participation

* Membership at the Golden Anniversary Year is in the Appendix.

which could evolve from this spirit was the vital factor in any company's daily life, and Joe Foster was very much aware of it.

"I don't know how to thank you for it," he told the Twenty-five-Year Club members that night. "I've given it some thought and I've decided that each one of you will receive a ten-dollar award for each year you've been with the company."

This came as a surprise to the members. It might also have been a surprise to Joe Foster. Though the total came to sixty thousand dollars, this was the sort of thing Joe Foster would do impulsively. He had done it before.

One Saturday, some Foster Grant executives went to a football game at the Leominster field, and they had the occasion to complain several times about the difficulty of seeing the score on the small scoreboard at the far end of the field. Monday morning, during a business conference with Joe Foster, the subject of the game came up, and somebody mentioned the scoreboard, commenting that something ought to be done about it. Joe said, "Then let's do something. Let's put in a better one. Look into it, will you? Find out who makes scoreboards and have somebody put in a good one. Send the bill to my office." The bill came to thirty-five hundred dollars.

Like Sam, Joe Foster never ran for public office, but he was much more active in community affairs, often serving on civic committees and as chairman of fund-raising drives. Probably the most important of these for Joe Foster was the chairmanship of the committee which raised half a million dollars to convert a movie house into the Leominster Recreation Center. This was a lot of money to raise in a town of about thirty thousand people, but the job was done in a year. Serving on the committee were some of Sam's old friends, including Lionel Kavanaugh, Louis Levine, and Charles Dentrs, and they, like the whole town, agreed that it was Joe Foster's energetic leadership that brought about success so quickly and so thoroughly.

The family spirit of mutual aid and assistance among Foster Grant personnel was instrumental in the organization of a credit union in 1937. In the Golden Anniversary Year it had reserves of almost three million dollars.

Among the organizers of the credit union was P. J. Byrnes. He had gone to work for Foster Grant on St. Patrick's Day, 1936, for twenty-five cents an hour and, like everybody else, he did all kinds of jobs He was in on the move to North Main Street; he worked on a bench and in shipping. One day while a hurricane was blowing the roof off the building, Byrnes was up there hammering the roof down. In 1941, when the company acquired it first IBM machines, Byrnes was put in charge. During the Golden Anniversary Year he was in charge of Sunglass Customer Service.

Byrnes has said, "This company is a big family affair. A feeling of belonging is expected and everybody here has it. One night when I was working late Joe Foster happened to pass my office, and he looked in and asked, 'Hey, Byrnes, do you need all these lights?' He was letting me know that he appreciated the extra hours, but in his joking way he was reminding me that the company's electric bills were my business as much as his."

Sam and Joe Foster were the first two members of the

credit union when it was formed. The company had about two hundred employees then, most of whom also joined, and within a year the credit union had over two thousand dollars. Then an assistant treasurer absconded with it all, and everything had to be started afresh. From then on, the fund grew steadily; over the next thirty years it has been both a stimulant to regular and habitual saving and thrift and an economical source of borrowing for everything from buying homes to buying Easter clothes, from paying hospital bills to paying for vacation trips.

Another man very much aware of the family spirit at Foster Grant was the man who had contributed so much to it. He was Zarmair Shepherd—Sheppy to everyone. Armenian by birth, Sheppy was raised in Turkey. He came from a theatrical family and had himself won fame as a child actor, but his father wanted a more stable life for him and saw to it that Sheppy was well educated. Sheppy came to America in 1922. A gifted linguist, he could speak seven languages, and his intention was to do social work among immigrants. This was a narrow field with little job opportunity, and thus Sheppy's first years in this country were lean ones.

In 1925, he saw a want ad in the papers: H. Goodman & Sons were looking for factory workers. Hundreds of men applied for the few jobs. They jammed the lobby of the building. They lined the staircase to the personnel office on the second floor. They poured out onto the street. As time passed, they turned into a hostile and impatient mob. Fights broke out. Sheppy, a small, slight man, with a gentle nature, waited two hours. Then he faced the fact that he had no factory experience and probably wouldn't be hired anyway, and he left. He had gone a few steps down the street when he saw two men come out of what looked like a service entrance to the factory. Sheppy grabbed the door before it shut and went inside.

Immediately he was stopped by a burly man who demanded, "What the hell are you doing here?"

"I'm looking for a job," Sheppy said.

"Well, this isn't the personnel office," the man said. "Down the block, at the main entrance."

"I know," said Sheppy. "I've been there. There are too many men on the line already. I wouldn't even get interviewed."

"That's your tough luck," the man said. "Now, get out of here. This area is for authorized personnel only."

Sheppy said, "I'm sorry if I troubled you." And he turned to go.

"Hey, wait," the man called. "Would you take a job sweeping floors?"

"I would."

"I'm the foreman of this section, and that's the only job I've got for anybody. You can have it."

"I'll take it. Thank you."

"I want to tell you something," the man said. "In my whole life, you're the first person who's ever said 'I'm sorry' to me for anything."

"I'm glad I did," said Sheppy.

Thus Sheppy went to work for the Goodmans as a floor sweeper. In a few weeks, he was assigned to cleaning the oily machinery. A few weeks after that, he was operating a machine. A leading Goodman item was a metal hair-curler.

By 1932, Sheppy was foreman of that section. It was then decided to move this operation to Foster Grant, and Sheppy went to Leominster on loan to train workers. In the Golden Anniversary Year, he was still there.

Sheppy could never bear inactivity. He had been in Leominster just a few months when he asked Sam Foster if it would be all right for him to organize bowling teams among the employees. It would be. Then came baseball teams and basketball teams. One day Sheppy went to Sam and said, "I've talked it over with some of the other workers, and we think it would be fun to put on a play. Is that all right with you?"

"Sure," said Sam. "Go ahead."

"When we're ready, can we give the performances up on the fourth floor?" Sheppy asked.

"I've got a better idea," Sam said. "When you're ready, let's rent one of the movie houses downtown. That way, you can give your performance in a regular theater." The plays became an annual event, with Sheppy as director.

Sheppy was appalled to learn that, though Leominster was just fifty miles from Boston, there were many people at Foster Grant who had never gone into the city to see a Broadway show or attend a symphony concert. One complaint was the long round-trip drive in a single evening; another was the cost of the evening in town. For Sheppy, these events were the stuff of life.

Sheppy got an idea which he first cleared with the Fosters and then went into Boston to carry out. He was able to get discounts on theater and concert tickets by buying them in quantity, like a theater party, and he also made a similar discount arrangement with a good restaurant. Then he lined up buses to provide the round-trip transportation. Thus for a price below the cost of the ticket, employees got a night on the town—with culture.

On the first occasion of a Foster Grant theater party, Sheppy instituted what became another tradition. Before the buses left Leominster, he canvassed them with coin canisters, asking for donations. He did this on each subsequent excursion, whether it was to the theater, a concert, an athletic event, the ice show, the circus, or just a picnic at some historic site. At the end of the year, he presented a tally of the collection to Joe Foster. Sheppy was pleased but not surprised when Joe Foster wrote a check for the same amount and gave it to him. A committee of employees then decided which local charity or civic project or institution would receive the total as a gift from the people who worked at Foster Grant.

Before long, scarcely a week passed without some special event at the plant; scarcely a month passed without a trip somewhere. A long weekend in New York became a regular excursion; so did a week in Washington, D.C. Sheppy arranged mystery trips—people got on the bus without knowing where they were going or what they would do when they got there. To get more money for the annual donation, Sheppy persuaded movie houses in Leominster and Fitchburg to let him sell cut-rate tickets daily in the Foster Grant cafeteria, with a dime for each ticket going into his canisters.

Sheppy's role as the Foster Grant recreation director just grew, like Topsy, and before he knew it he was spending most of his free time planning events, supervising them, and cleaning up afterwards. When he learned there was a national association of industrial recreation directors, he joined it and attended its conferences, hoping to pick up ideas for new events at Foster Grant. Instead, it seemed that Sheppy was the one who came up with the new ideas. The association awarded him a citation for his full program at Foster Grant. As much as this meant to him, there was something that meant more.

He said this, "I am the recreation director for Foster Grant, yes—but that's not all. I work here. I've got a job, and I'm proud of it. I run the tool crib."

❋　❋　❋　❋

Sam Foster withdrew from the Foster Grant Company in 1942. But he did not go into retirement. At fifty-nine, Sam still considered himself a young man, still full of ideas and plans for the future. Now he wanted the time and the freedom to carry out the ideas and pursue the plans. A financial settlement was made for his interests in Foster Grant, and the management passed to Joe Foster and the Goodmans. Sam Foster moved to Los Angeles.

And he immediately launched a number of new careers. Real estate transactions had always fascinated him. With his brothers Harry and Maurice, he formed a realty company and started to buy up apartment houses and hotels. Sam also opened a string of self-service gas stations. He acquired interests in shopping centers and industrial land development sites. He remained an inventor and obtained a patent on a parking garage which overcame the familiar problem of a long wait for service. In Sam's garage, cars were not parked, as such, but "filed" by a system of cranes which could also retrieve a car from its position in an "open shelf" building within seconds.

In 1966, Sam Foster formulated a plan that had been on his mind for sixty years. It was probably the most ambitious effort of his life, and he was ready to put his personal fortune into it. Sam Foster wanted to turn America into one big family—and he knew how it could be done.

In a prospectus Sam prepared, he said:

"For most of recorded history, the basic unit of social living has been the family. A family unit—not just mother, father, and children, but grandparents, unmarried aunts and uncles, far-removed cousins—was a group which could, and did, face every crisis and survive. Within the family, there was always a helping hand, a meaningful place for the elderly, a word of advice or encouragement for the young. Now land becomes scarcer and houses grow smaller. Modern corporations send their young executives from city to city. Family units, in terms of a large group of related persons, no longer exist. Young mothers rely on Dr. Spock and each other instead of their own mothers or other older relatives. Grandparents are relegated to a weekly 'duty letter' home. Many individuals, old and young, feel alienated from their society and no longer know that they are secure within a tightly knit group of family.

"Perhaps one way of aiding in this situation would be to provide and to encourage the growth of a new type of 'family unit.' The actual blood relationship is not the important element in establishing this grouping; the feeling of security provided by the close group makes the 'family.' "

Sam envisioned this: a network of community centers across the country, each truly the center of the community. In a sense, each would be a recreation center, in that each would have a swimming pool, a gym, rooms for other sports and club meetings. But each center would have lounges of various sizes where people could just sit around and talk. Sam said:

"These centers would then provide a meeting place for rich and poor, young and old alike, within a given neighborhood. Senior citizens, rich in the knowledge and experience gained in living, would be available to share this wealth with those who are in need of a kind word and friendly advice. Children who are eager for learning experiences and constructive activity would have their energies and talents directed into useful channels. Busy, harried mothers could find others to talk to, advice and, most of all, a few moments of quiet and relaxation. All would find the companionship which enriches lives. It is hoped that this companionship would not be limited but would cut across the barriers of age, ethnic groupings, and other artificial stumbling blocks."

Above all, Sam wanted everybody in the community to be actively involved in the center. He felt that each center should be able to meet the needs of a thousand families— about five thousand people—within a specific area. Each family would be registered in a census that would show personal interests and business activities as well as age and sex. This way, people of common interests and common problems could be led to each other. A keynote in Sam's plan was to make people of the neighborhood available to each other, because through this open communication the gaps which separate people could be bridged.

Without being an employment agency, the center would know about available jobs in the community and would know about people seeking jobs. Without being a welfare agency, the center would have an emergency fund to meet the sudden financial needs that often pop up. Without being a counseling service, the center would be able to arrange for personal and professional counseling by getting the person who needed the advice to the person whose personal and professional experiences qualified him to give it. The center would not replace any public or private agencies active in these areas but would supplement them, and on a voluntary basis.

Sam believed that participation in a center's activities on a volunteer basis would be its life's blood. There could be a sense of family in the center and in the neighborhood only when everybody freely and selflessly extended to others the thoughtfulness, concern, attention, and time required for harmonious living in a good home. Sam therefore recommended that the paid staff of each center be kept small. The programs in each center should, Sam felt, be carried out by the people themselves. He said:

"The programming needs of each center will depend entirely upon the needs of the population served by each. Some centers might find themselves with few senior citizens and large numbers of young people; therefore, such centers would have to concentrate on job training and child care.

Others might have populations composed almost entirely of senior citizens; certainly, then, the programming needs will be different.

"However, the basic purposes of the center would remain the same, no matter the composition of its membership. The purpose of the center is to provide a place and people to meet the social and economic needs of its membership. Membership is automatic and free; participation in the program is voluntary. Every person living within the geographical area served by the center is a member, and individual needs will be taken into account when the center arranges its programming.

"The purpose of the center is to help provide an answer to the sweeping social revolutions of our times, to enable the individual to find a comfortable place for himself in the rapidly changing environment around him.

"The center should provide more than job training; it should provide, in a sense, life training for the young people who come to it. It might, in a sense, serve as a 'substitute family' for those who are alone or alienated from their own homes.

"A further purpose of the centers would be to aid those who must move from one section of the country to another and who find themselves lost and alone among new surroundings. Centers at each end of the move would be prepared to facilitate the relocation for their members by referring them to the center which will then serve them and by providing such other assistance as is necessary and possible."

Sam Foster felt this way:

"As the society around us changes, the needs of the

individuals within that society change even more rapidly and violently. We are now in a transition period, when new forms of living together must be developed. Family-unit ties have been broken or greatly disturbed by the greater mobility of our population, by the ever increasing longevity of our senior citizens, by the rapid change of our society from its rural base to an urban one, by the growing gulf between the generations caused by the rapid physical changes in our world. Minority groups are demanding, more insistently than ever before, their rightful share of the good things our lives and times have to offer us.

"New patterns must be established to meet these new needs. Through the creation of family-neighborhood centers, just such a new pattern of group—or family—living might be established. There would be a place where the individual could go for help with his problems and for recognition of his worth as a person. Senior citizens and young men and women just beginning their active lives could find areas of common interest and ways in which to communicate with each other.

"The problems of alienation and loneliness could find new solutions through a sharing of needs and satisfactions made possible by a neighborhood group. As the family unit, at one time, met these needs, so now a larger 'family' would exist to provide a stable foundation for the growth of the individual.

"Such a group could indeed serve as a substitute family for those who need such help. Others might find new paths to self-sufficiency or could at least be given the incentives to try.

"Certainly such centers could aid young people in determining their own standards of right and wrong and could assist them in finding worthwhile outlets for their energies. It could provide them with a sense of belonging which is of such particular importance to young people, as indeed it is to each one of us; and without trying to take over the place of organized religion, it could try to point the way to useful, full lives.

"Senior citizens would find places for themselves in such endeavors by bringing to bear their experiences so painfully garnered over the years. Old and young have much to offer each other, if only the paths of communication are opened. This development of communication and sharing would be one of the main functions of the centers.

"Other functions, of course, would be to fulfill special needs of individuals, which will vary from center to center, from area to area. Young mothers would be taught ways of rearing their children which would enable the family to grow more happily. Women who must manage their homes with limited funds could be shown the ways of preparing wholesome, attractive meals which would not exceed their budgets. The volunteer staff might also provide a baby-sitting service to young families who cannot afford such help but who require it desperately. Men and women whose hobbies or professions have given them valuable skills and abilities will be able to share them with those who are in need of such instruction and help.

"The centers, as such, would in no way attempt to compete with the already existing aid institutions within a given area, nor would they attempt to compete with the exciting new programs being developed. The centers are not primarily methods of extending financial assistance, nor are they basically vocational training schools. Both of these efforts are a part of the entire program to be offered by the centers, but not the heart of it.

"The centers would supplement these activities and would offer a home to those who have no other place to go.

"They would offer a pattern of living to those whose lives are aimless and would help each of us to help himself—and those around us."

❁ ❁ ❁ ❁

In his prospectus, Sam said:

"I arrived as a penniless immigrant to this country and, after a relatively short time, became the owner of a small manufacturing company. This company is known now as Foster Grant, Inc., of Leominster, Massachusetts. I had help at every step of my way and I feel that the time has now come for me to repay my indebtedness to this great society of ours by extending help to those all around me who are in such dire need of a friend, a kind word, encouragement and aid.

"Whether or not my name is attached to this plan is of no real importance. What is important is that this plan come into being as a living symbol of those ideals which have helped to make this country so great. What is equally important is that all of us have this opportunity to work together to help each other—and so to help all of us.

"I believe this plan may better the lot of all Americans. I am eager to start the wheels in motion. If even a portion of the proposal can be put into actual practice, I shall die in peace."

* * * *

Samuel C. Foster, Jr., died in Los Angeles on February 27, 1966. He was eighty-two years old.

* * * *

Preparing the prospectus was Sam Foster's last major endeavor. When he was satisfied with the text, he dictated two letters to men he felt might be willing to help get the project started. One man was John William Gardner, then Secretary of the U.S. Department of Health, Education and Welfare, and director of President Johnson's War on Poverty. The other was Richard N. Goodwin, a White House aide. To Goodwin, Sam wrote:

"In September, 1965, *Nation's Business* published an article entitled 'A Pause Would Be Refreshing,' written by Mr. Peter Lisagor. In that article, he quoted you as urging citizens of this country to submit ideas and suggestions for the betterment of our society. You asked for help in improving 'the quality of our lives.'

"The plan which I am submitting herewith is, of course, just a preliminary suggestion. I am sure that the expert opinion which you have available to you will help you to modify and strengthen the proposal. This proposal represents the results of sixty years of thought and planning. It is my fervent hope that this plan, for the people and of the people, may be operated in their best interests."

After Sam's death, his secretary told Joe Foster about the prospectus and the two letters that had been dictated but not as yet typed. Joe read the prospectus. He told the secretary to go ahead and type up the letters. In a cover letter, Joe Foster explained why the two letters were not signed.

Joe Foster kept a copy of the prospectus on his desk. He got to know it by heart, but even so, he would glance at its pages from time to time. In the Golden Anniversary Year, Joe Foster said, "Maybe someday we'll go ahead and build one for him."

9

Sam Foster never liked loose ends of any kind. When the company first moved out to North Main Street, most of the sixty-five acres was undeveloped, and whenever Sam looked out the window at all that empty space he got the feeling that he was on the moon. To remedy this, Sam had a fence installed around the office and factory buildings, then had the enclosed area landscaped, thus creating a specific identity for the company out there in the wilderness. Just beyond the fence was a dirt road that ran fifty yards to the west to Main Street. Sam didn't like this, either. "I can't see who's coming," he complained. He had the road shut off and had a driveway built from the office door northward some two hundred yards across the field to Hamilton Street. This satisfied Sam, and he said, "Now we won't have any surprise visitors."

At the time, Joe Foster feared they might lose a few visitors in the vastness of the former piano factory, and Sam had assured him that one day they would need even more space. That day came sooner than anybody expected.

One day Joe Foster got a telephone call from Abe Goodman at his New Jersey office. The Goodmans were looking for a container for a hair-setting lotion they were about to bring out, and somehow this need came to the attention of two young scientists who had a small plant a few miles away. They brought Abe Goodman a sample of a polyethylene plastic bottle they were making by blow-molding on a machine they had developed. Goodman told Joe Foster that the bottle was exceptionally good. He also said that he got the impression that the two scientists were starving. Goodman suggested that Joe Foster call on the young men and find out if there was any way Foster Grant could help them.

Joe went to the plant. It was about the size of a two-car garage. There was only one machine. Joe Foster found out that the small company had only one customer. They gave Joe a demonstration. The machine was crude and needed many improvements, but even so, it could turn out quality work. Then Joe asked how Foster Grant could help. The way was obvious: the two men needed money. Joe Foster offered to put up money on a partnership basis.

While the details were being worked out, and while Joe Foster was debating whether to expand the plant in New Jersey or move the equipment to Leominster, a competing firm filed suit against the two scientists for infringement of its patent for blow-molding. The plaintiff lost the suit and also lost an appeal. By then, however, these two scientists decided they really didn't want to remain in the bottle business, and they offered to sell out. Foster Grant bought.

Now that Foster Grant was in the bottle-making business, Joe Foster decided to call on the company's only customer. This was Celebrity, Inc., of New York, recently started by Jack Unger. Celebrity, Inc., was then packaging travel kits and cosmetic articles. Jack Unger was delighted with the news that the New Jersey plant had been acquired by Foster Grant and had been moved to Leominster. Joe told him that Foster Grant engineers were already improving the original machine, and also making new machines that would allow for a greater variety of production. This, too, was good news for Jack Unger because it meant he could expand his own line.

During the conversation, Unger gave Joe Foster an order that amounted to several thousand dollars. Joe wrote it out, and then the two men resumed their conversation about their plans for their companies. When Joe got up to leave, a scene occurred that had happened so often it was becoming traditional with Foster Grant customers.

Jack Unger reached for his checkbook. "How much of a deposit do you want, Joe?"

"You don't have to give me a deposit," Joe said.

Jack Unger shrugged. "Well, all right, but I've never had this happen to me before."

Joe asked, "You're going to pay your bill, aren't you?"

"Sure."

"That's all I have to know."

Unger asked, "Don't you want to take a look at my financial statement?"

Joe Foster shook his head. "No. If I did, you might want to take a look at mine."

They both laughed and shook hands.

In the Golden Anniversary Year, Celebrity, Inc., was still a Foster Grant customer.

*　*　*　*

The place was getting a little crowded. All four floors of the former piano factory were now being used for production, storage, and offices. The office building had been enlarged to three times its original size. The Research and Development building, which was once a shack, now looked like a hangar. The polymerization plant, repeatedly expanded to accommodate the large equipment, eventually gave the impression that Rube Goldberg had been the architect. The empty acreage began to disappear.

If Joe Foster was apprehensive about the move to the piano factory, he had no hesitation about the next Foster Grant acquisition. He had come to the conclusion that, in terms of company growth, there was no end in sight for

Foster Grant. Foster Grant had become No. 1 in the country in sunglasses. In chemicals, *Barron's* magazine listed Foster Grant as right on the heels of the giants.

All these circumstances made additional space essential, and Joe Foster found it in Manchester, New Hampshire. The building stood on the banks of the Merrimack River and had previously been occupied by a shoe manufacturer. The place was gigantic. It had a capacity of four hundred thousand square feet. Adjoining was a huge power plant, and Joe Foster had plans for it. After the transaction was completed in 1956, the bottle-making equipment was moved in. So were parts of the sunglasses and combs departments temporarily, to ease the space shortage in Leominster. At the power plant, equipment began to arrive which would one day turn out a new type of nylon, a project Joe Foster had patiently been coaxing along for years.

By the Golden Anniversary Year, chemical sales comprised almost forty percent of the Foster Grant earnings. This was far greater than anyone expected; but then, few people expected the plastics industry to take off the way it did. Joe Foster was one man who did foresee the tremendous potentials in plastics, and this was why he was ready to forge ahead in the field at a time when a mistake would have meant financial catastrophe. As a result, the Golden Anniversary Year of 1969 found Foster Grant with an impressive array of successful products.

—Fostarene. This general purpose polystyrene is a hard, rigid plastic which is crystal clear in its natural form and may be produced in various colors and transparencies. When, in fact, the Foster Grant color-blending laboratory was developed in 1959 and could reproduce any color of the rainbow the sales of colored polystyrene almost doubled. Fostarene is one of the lightest in weight of the rigid plastics and can be formed to virtually any shape and to close tolerance. It is odorless. It is widely used in toys, housewares, packaging, combs, refrigerator parts, and for various applications in the electronics industry.

—Fosta Tuf-Flex. This member of the polystyrene family is a "graft-type" rubber-modified polymer that has outstanding impact resistance. Commonly referred to as high-impact polystyrene, it is made by combining styrene and rubber. The toughness, flexibility, and impact strength of Fosta Tuf-Flex recommends its use in a wide variety of products, since it can be molded easily and lends itself readily to extrusion into sheets. A major market for Tuf-Flex is in the household appliance field, where it is used for refrigerator liners, radio and air conditioner housings. Tuf-Flex also is being used for food containers, particularly for dairy products, disposable cups and dishes, and for toys.

—Fosta Foam. In 1966, Foster Grant began producing expandable polystyrene beads, sometimes called foam. This process is unique in that the polymerized styrene beads contain a foaming agent and are expanded by steam before they are fed into a closed mold. Steam is then injected into the mold, fusing the beads and forming the finished shape of the product. The result is a product of lower density than one formed by the commonly used injection molding process in which the beads are melted rather than fused. Foster Grant entered the expandable bead market with resin types designed to place the company in both the block molding market and the custom packaging market. Molded blocks are cut into specific sizes for use as low-temperature insulation in refrigeration, flotation billets, and perimeter and cavity wall insulation for construction. End products of custom molding include such items as coffee cups, typewriter cases, boats, children's toys, ice buckets, and instrument cases.

—Fosta Net. Another expandable beads product, the netting is formed by extrusion molding from two counter-rotating dies, resulting in a light, tough, and strong substance that provides excellent protective packaging.

—Fosta Nylon. Originally, Nylon 6—the type Foster Grant produces at Manchester—found its major outlets in molding and monofilament applications. While these areas continued to provide a sound core of business, it was the newer avenue of extrusion that generated excitement for the product. Nylon 6 was easier to process than the older, traditional Nylon 6/6. It vacuum-formed readily. It was tough. These properties led Fosta Nylon into a number of new areas. Extruded into wire jacketing, it found widespread military and civilian use. As tubing, it turned up in new automobiles as speedometer and brake cables. Extruded into film and coated onto other plastics, it was being used to package processed meats and cheese. And by itself nylon film was being made into bags in which frozen foods could be boiled.

—Specialty chemicals. Among the important specialty chemicals produced at Baton Rouge are divinylbenzene (DVB), which, like the styrene monomer, is used in ion exchange resins and synthetic rubber; and Fosta-Sol, an aromatic vinyl which is a major ingredient in polyester and alkyd resins.

—In the Golden Anniversary Year, Foster Grant scientists were in the last stages of developing the company's own acrylonitrile-butadiene-styrene (ABS) resin. This relatively new plastic was already widely accepted by industry for its excellent processability, impact resistance, good heat stability, hardness, low temperature performance, and overall environmental resistance. The automobile industry was using ABS for instrument clusters, arm rests, and kick panels, and experimentation was going on to determine its suitability in auto grilles. Also, the appliance, industrial pipe, and luggage industries provided a steadily increasing outlet for the new resin.

This product growth in just a dozen years, the unchallenged leadership in sunglasses achieved during the same period, and the expanding requests for custom molding all combined to create a festive air at Foster Grant in the Golden Anniversary Year. The excitement was beamed in two directions—to the past, of which everyone could be proud, and to the future, for which everyone could be confident.

    ✿   ✿   ✿   ✿

This growth indicated to Joseph Foster that a gradual reorganization of the company was necessary in order to handle the immediately foreseeable expansion and to plan for the future and inevitably the perpetuation of the company and its policies and its programs.

As a first step, Joe Foster foresaw the need for a wider sales coverage. Therefore, he began to build a Polymer Sales group to work in coordination with the Muehlstein staff. In line with this, there also began the training of a larger service group to work with the customers who were buying Foster's polymer products in greater quantities and for ever increasing uses.

As the sales grew from this greater marketing effort, the company expanded its markets from what principally had been the Eastern seaboard to the Midwest and even Far West. It established a plant in Peru, Illinois, for the polymerization of its plastics. This assured better services to customers in that area and inevitably resulted in more volume. Again, this required boosting the capacity of the Baton Rouge monomer plant and adopting new shipping methods for economical and faster delivery of the monomer to both Peru and Leominster.

To explore the market on the West Coast, Foster Grant acquired an interest in Baum Chemical Company which it, subsequently, acquired in toto. This firm, under the management of Dr. Sidney Baum, former vice president of Foster Grant, is now a principal supplier of styrene sheet in the area. As Foster Grant broadens its market, it will probably become the focal point for a polymerization plant and perhaps even for a monomer facility.

Joe Foster has always been a marketing man, and he early recognized the great future in packaging for plastics. Accordingly, when the opportunity presented itself, he acquired the Wilson Plastic Co. in Sandusky, Ohio, which at that time was just entering the cottage cheese container field. This company has since expanded considerably and is now one of the principal suppliers of such plastic containers in the country. Here, too, it is diversifying and is beginning to develop containers for many other products.

To make sure that the company will perpetuate itself and continue to grow, Joe Foster and the Goodmans arranged for a stock issue which made the company a truly public corporation. Elected the first officers of the corporation were:

Abraham Goodman, Chairman and Treasurer

Joseph C. Foster, President

Robert O. Purvin, Executive Vice President

Jacob Goodman, Vice Chairman

Jacob Chatkis, Vice President and Secretary

and as Vice Presidents:

Sidney J. Baum

Milton W. Bernstein

Raymond J. Hartigan

F. Drew Mayfield

To keep up with this growth, the company adopted a divisional structure. The principal divisions and the executives in charge are:

Chemical and Resins—David Markowitz

Consumer Products—Charles H. Loiselle

Converted Products—William A. Myers

Each of these divisions has shown a very fine growth and has developed its own management corps in depth. With that achieved, Joe Foster felt that there was only one remaining chore to fill, and that was to elect a successor to himself so that he could be free to devote his time almost exclusively to the future development of the company and to divorce himself from its everyday affairs.

For ten years, Joe Foster searched for a good man with

the intellectual, emotional, and professional capacities to cope with the labyrinth of administrative detail the presidency of the company had become. Then Joe found him. He was Edward Creiger, a senior partner in Creiger, Singer and Lusardi, a Worcester accounting firm formerly known as Baker and Baker. The firm had been fiscal advisers to Foster Grant for many years, and Ed Creiger had handled the account. He not only possessed all the necessary capacities for the presidency of Foster Grant, but he already had a working knowledge of the company, having conferred with Joe Foster on numerous policy decisions.

* * * *

The Foster Grant story is, because of the nature of the company, a story about people, the people who comprise the Foster Grant family, both employees and customers. The company's annual reports vividly demonstrate the inventiveness and incentiveness which have put Foster Grant among the leaders in American industry. The purpose of this book is to honor the men and women who have made it all possible.

Directors
and
Officers